**WILLIAM WARD WATKIN** FAIA PROFESSOR OF ARCHITECTURE THE RICE INSTITUTE

# PLANNING AND BUILDING THE MODERN CHURCH

**F. W. DODGE CORPORATION** NEW YORK 1951

# CONTENTS

# EVOLUTION OF MODERN CHURCH PLANNING, 1900-1950

We are beginning a great and meaningful period of church building. Architects, clergymen, and laymen alike are seeking to plan and build modern churches which will inspire reverence and be worthy of permanence. It is very significant that work of a new and inviting character in the design of churches has been developed during the past two or three decades. This encourages us to look forward toward the gradual development of a great modern art suitable to the church and suitable to our age.

We have come to an age in church building which will admit the validity of modern scholarship. Until very recently churchmen have accepted the modern forms with reservation, while awaiting the fulfillment of qualities distinctly appropriate to the church. Skill supported by serious thinking and sensitive study is required to produce structures of great meaning. In the field of church building we find these qualities developing and promising to achieve a rich reality worthy of the church.

The evolution of church planning through the first half of this century was stimulated by a clear need for churches of greater usefulness and beauty than those of the nineteenth century. With the opening of the twentieth century came a sincere effort to advance the design of our churches so that they would be fitting to our maturing civilization. During the nineteenth century we in America had experienced the so-called Gothic revival, and later the revival of Romanesque form. The leaders of these movements produced churches that attained considerable national interest, but the skills of these leaders did not survive and flourish among their followers. Church building became a declining rather than an advancing art, and its forms became increasingly dull.

At the beginning of this century such leaders as Charles D. Maginnis and Ralph Adams Cram were writing in a serious manner, with courage and enthusiasm, concerning church building in America. Throughout the preceding generation population growth through migration and immigration had established new and uncertain conditions throughout large areas of the country. Churches which had been built were of an essentially temporary nature, being neither adequate nor distinctive buildings. The degree of Christian scholarship of architects, clergymen and laymen was not sufficiently advanced to attain churches of refinement and beauty. In opposition to such conditions these men saw fit to write their inspiring papers; Maginnis writing of the problems of the Catholic Church, Cram of the problems of the Protestant Church. It is difficult for us today to consider these efforts as modern in nature, but nevertheless, they repre-

1

sented the spirit of searching for design in church building that led America out of the morass of dullness in which it had been floundering.

I can recall the articles by Ralph Adams Cram appearing in *The Churchman* as early as 1905. They were a series of short articles presented in a charming manner, which set forth the problems of church building as he saw them  He sought to accent the traditions of the Church of England by English churches, large and small; churches of stone, churches with towers, but on the whole rather quiet buildings without excessive ornament. The examples presented for illustration were small country churches of scale appropriate to the average parish churches then being planned in our country. By the brilliance of Bertram Goodhue's pen and ink drawings, the designs of Cram were given a reality which stirred the imagination of both clergy and architects, and which by 1910 led to the beginning of an active period in modern church design.

Mr. Maginnis, on the other hand, suggested that architects study the splendid brick churches of Lombardy. Brick was a very generally used material throughout American cities and towns. Good brick work, appropriate to their building needs, was appearing in industrial and commercial buildings. In church work it was being poorly used with rather horrible results.

Both of these architects sincerely desired to build modern churches. Neither of them was deliberately trying to rebuild historical edifices—buildings which had retained beauty and inspiration from the past, but could not be works of the twentieth century. Instead, they felt that traditional values which they themselves held very high should be understood by persistent study. This approach could inspire a beauty of architecture in the church building of our own country which would be a direct development of the great values of the past. Perhaps the fact that it would take decades to achieve again the noble qualities of such buildings was obscured by their great enthusiasm. The several decades which have followed the periods of their writing have proved this to be true.

At the opening of the century the most generally accepted and prevailing church building form throughout America was that of the Georgian or Colonial type meeting house. The simplicity of the brick or the wooden churches of earlier times, existing in the towns and cities of the Atlantic seaboard, held a warm historic meaning and a welcome acceptance for our people. This influence continues to be very real today.

In the decade which preceded the coming of World War I, very important works were begun and carried to completion along the lines suggested by Maginnis and Cram. The church architects were seeking to study in detail the nature of the Gothic buildings of England, and the nature of the Romanesque buildings of Italy. Travel abroad and reference to available historic documents made the form of these fields of historic architecture partially known within the offices of the architects. The succeeding stages had much of the superficiality which characterizes a fashion or fad. Inappropriate collection of detail replaced substantial solution of structure, and the movement became one of declining value.

One of the major points emphasized by Goodhue, and expressed frequently in his work, was not understood sufficiently to direct the progress of the church architect. This spirit of Goodhue is indicated in the most impressive of the earlier works of the firm of Cram, Goodhue, and Ferguson, (page 3) which stands on the hillside overlooking the Hudson at West Point, New York. From the day of its completion the Cadet Chapel has been an inspiring gem of strong Christian architecture embodying Christian ideals. The success of the solution is in its fitness to its location; its stonework characteristic of the stone cliffs on which it rests; its sturdiness of proportion, yet with loftiness adequate for its inspiring interior. Simple almost to the point of pure geometry, it omits useless Gothic

*Cadet Chapel, United States Military Academy. Cram, Goodhue and Ferguson, Architects. Photo by Major W. W. Watkin Jr.*

detail, copied inappropriately from England or France, and is built with assurance and conviction, guided by the creative mind of Goodhue and his amazing skill. The Cadet Chapel records a thorough understanding in architectural terms of the degree to which it is proper for our modern buildings to be influenced by traditional form. It carries the intellectual strength of an able thesis, proving clearly that beauty can be recaptured and fully expressed without clinging to historic detail. It proves that strong, sturdy buildings of good proportion and of high artistic interest constitute a creative architecture in our own land as well as elsewhere. Had we grasped, as Goodhue did, this understanding of simplicity and strength, and had we then developed skills suitable to it, we would not have had to face the continued criticism that building in traditional form has failed to reach creative mastery. The criticism has been valid.

Throughout the years immediately preceding World War I, church building showed a continuous and remarkable increase both in numbers and in extent. Beautiful churches were completed in the cities of the East, throughout the cities of the Middle West, and in the cities of the Pacific Coast. The Church of St. Thomas was brought to completion in New York, Calvary Church in Pittsburgh, and St. Paul's Church in Los Angeles. Throughout the entire country the offices of architects were making sketches and preliminary plans for new churches. The study of the forms of the Romanesque and Gothic churches of Europe was showing direct influence on the work of these architects. Such churches as had been built by the firms of Maginnis and Walsh; Cram, Goodhue, and Ferguson; Hobart Upjohn; Henry Vaughn; Myron Hunt; and Frank Watson were becoming

3

*Presbyterian Church, New Rochelle, New York. Eggers and Higgins, Architects. Photo by Gottscho-Schleisner*

known to architects throughout the country. However, the period before the coming of World War I was too short for the maturing of a clear understanding of the possibilities of tradition, coordinated with care and appropriateness to our American work. Here and there an architect was able to grasp with thoroughness the possible creative artistry suggested by the styles of the past, but this was the exception rather than the rule.

Following World War I, we in America soon became aware of a new and unusual manner of design in church building which was appearing throughout the countries of Western Europe. For the peoples of those countries, the great churches were churches that had been built in the distant past. In recent generations religious architecture had been of a very poor type. Because of this discrepancy, and because of post-war economic conditions, it was most natural that the church building forms which followed World War I should be very different from those which had immediately preceded it. The architects could not build churches such as had been built in the very distant past, and they could not accept as valid such churches as had been built by recent generations. Above all, their work was controlled by rigid economy.

M. André Lurçat was a truthful exponent of the law of economy under which Europe had to work. He emphasized this principle by saying that it was always dangerous in architecture to pass willfully beyond economy: "From the beginning to the end of our work, the law of economy is respected."

The post-war churches of Holland, Denmark and Sweden were more attractive than those of France and Italy. Churches through the northern countries were very generally built of brick, with interesting forms developed in their detail. In France and Italy, concrete, an alluring material, came into the post-war church building. Over in Germany, combinations of brick and concrete, closer to traditional form than in the other countries, developed some attractive features. The churches were, however, relatively heavy and dark, although abundantly expressive of permanence.

Here in America after the war, we returned to church building on a still broader and most costly basis. We were not bound by the forces of economy as were the architects of Europe. Therefore, traditional form and detail flourished far beyond any appropriate need. This tended to lower rather than raise our creative efforts in church architecture. The prevailing styles continued as before the war. The Byzantine tradition was embodied with unique beauty in St. Bartholomew's Church in New York by Bertram Goodhue. The Georgian tradition appeared with unusually graceful charm in the Presbyterian Church at New Rochelle, New York (page 4), the work of the office of Eggers and Higgins. The Spanish tradition gained in favor with such examples as Myron Hunt's First Congregational Church at Riverside, California. The Gothic tradition extended to many examples throughout the country, one of the most conspicuous being Allen and Collens' Riverside Church in New York.

Again the period of high activity lasted but a short time. With the depression of 1929 and 1930 economy became as important in America as it had been in post-war Europe. Church building came to a standstill. Such construction as was done was work of immediate need, limited in size and cost. These tragic conditions opened the eyes of the architects, clergymen and laymen to the possibilities of what we called modernism, which in truth was a simplified architecture forced upon us through economy. Its first forms in church building seemed quite inappropriate and often offensive; while in commercial fields many useful and desirable adaptations were being developed to a point of reasonable public acceptance.

The church architect had his opportunity to compose and use the non-traditional forms indicated by modern design. Here and there churches began to appear which had refinement and charm, yet were free from traditional detail. It is of these forms and of their further possibilities that we shall write in the following chapters of this book.

A widening of our vista in church building, accepting the capable artistry of modern forms, is appropriate. It becomes a challenge to the traditionalists to do good, clean, beautiful work, of fresh and vital form—to have their feet solidly on the ground and to work with methods normal to our time. The modernist, in turn, will do better work when he is challenged by able work on the part of the traditionalist. Both are striving to build the modern church and to make it functional and beautiful.

The modernists have demonstrated warm enthusiasm for their own work, which is not always justified in actual results. This enthusiasm itself is an excellent thing. I believe that it will bring similar attitude and a creative ability to those of more conservative or traditional leaning. We might expect that they too will give artistry to their work such as the modernists seek to give to theirs. This would mean bolder and cleaner walls of stone, handsomer and more carefully laid out walls of brick, freer and less coldly historic composition, and above all strength, simplicity, dignity, and charm. These can be attained as beautifully in conservative as in more modern form. Above all, we should not build confusion. Our work should be so skillfully done that it will create reverence appropriate to religion. It should be one more link in the very valuable chain that will lead us to unity of understanding.

A survey of church building such as can be found by searching through the architectural journals of the past thirty years will indicate very clearly that the church building has gradually become less dominant and less detached, while the church school and its attendant buildings have increased in size and importance. The result has been that the church group has grown greater in dimension. The opportunity of planning thus afforded has given greater importance to the entire composition. In the most modern examples, interesting and useful solutions have led to a freer and more creative vista. The greater usefulness and greater extent of these modern church plants cause both the architect and the churchmen to plan more carefully because of the greater expense involved.

The choice as to which should be built first, the church or the church school, is frequently imposed. Solutions of this problem are quite varied. For the entire plant, economy of space and of material are important. It is seldom possible to design without having these requirements constantly before us. Such extensive church plans were but little known at the opening of this century, and were still infrequent thirty years ago. Today we accept them as a normal requirement, and often go beyond the dimension which seemed adequate only a few years ago. We design our school and other buildings to provide flexibility for future use. This fact should lead intelligent architects to seek new compositions creating a high and churchly interest in the entire plant. These compositions can best avoid concentration, either stylistic or symbolic, upon the exterior of the church itself. Modern ornament in church work still evades the grasp of most of our modern designers. It is still severe at best, and has yet to attain popular approval. Certainly we have learned from the traditional enough to see that either the modern or the traditional will lose by frequent repetition or imitation. Wherever possible, each church should be an artistic creation, fitting to the particular site and serving and expressing the religious characteristics and requirements of the denomination for which it is built.

With this demand for a greater church plant, to do a more varied work and serve in a more continuous way the needs of its congregation, needless extravagances fall by the wayside. Towers, or at least elaborate towers, are less frequent. If they are appropriate, they can be quite simple, and far more attractive if not enriched with costly detail. Such direct and sensible reactions are becoming more general among our architects, among our clergymen and among our laymen. This shows a very healthy step in the right direction, and tends to bring a more complete understanding between these three groups of men. Only by cooperation, scholarship, and faithfulness to Christian ideals can good churches again be built and become a constant stimulus to high and noble endeavor among our people.

Some years ago I recorded my position concerning church building:

Creative design must be given freedom to compose and assemble materials and masses in a manner which shall record again our acceptance of the rightness of Christian emotion. Our churches deserve soundness of solution and beauty of expression. The church again must be understood as a problem, major and meaningful, in which a dignity of emotion is to be expressed and an atmosphere of quiet, contemplation, and consolation is to be achieved in terms and with materials consistent with our own day.*

This opinion was written before the coming of World War II. I hold it to be as true today as when it was written. The trends of the moment are far more liberal in acceptance of the non-traditional patterns than they have been at any time. They no longer abound with deliberate design of drastic change in order to command public attention. Sufficient modern building has accumulated in

* *The Church of Tomorrow,* Harper and Brothers, 1936

all lines except the church to widen our understanding of its building materials and forms.

The advancing level of prosperity throughout the entire nation should permit more building of new churches where they are needed to replace old churches than was possible twenty years ago. We must not treat this opportunity in a temporary manner; we must not treat the church as temporary in any sense. Each new building we must build with the hope that it will remain for generations and serve correctly its true purpose throughout that time. Its true purpose, more needed than ever, is a noble and united mission by which Christian civilization can be maintained and advanced, not alone in our country but throughout the entire world. In every field of building, be it industrial, commercial, or amusement, America is building buildings of greater dimension, greater cost, greater modern convenience and more attractive solution than it has ever built. We can do no less for the church.

During the few years that have followed the close of World War II, the amount of church building has increased steadily and the amount of proposed church building has increased amazingly, but the church as an institution has not held its primacy of importance. The need is greater now than ever before for architects, clergy, and laymen to join vigorously in their efforts to restore the high position of the church. This is not merely a professional obligation, but a religious, moral, and ethical obligation of our civilization.

The efforts of architects, clergymen and laymen throughout the half century from 1900 to 1950 have developed skills which will lead the church to regain its high primacy of meaning as expressed by splendid church buildings. These efforts have met repeated interruptions, as have our developments in material and social fields. They were interrupted by devastating wars and a world-wide economic depression. Their interruption is threatened by still further recurrence of war. However, the past half century has been marked by vast explorations in the field of science which open vistas of greater and greater opportunity. The problem immediately ahead of us all is that of applying intelligently the usefulness of our scientific and material gains in a manner which will aid us in declaring and developing the meaning of the church as the most essential philosophy of the future. It therefore becomes imperative that we develop an accumulating consciousness of the value of religious building and of religious art. Public attention to the essential nature of church building must be recovered in every city, town and village. It must proclaim both public interest and public pride in the lasting values of the church. In these values it transcends all other types of building. The greatest service that architecture can render to our age will be to intensify its every effort and its every ability to embody the church with enduring beauty.

Together the architect and the building committee plan and build the modern church. Its completeness and beauty when finished represent the mutual and enthusiastic work of these men.

The architect will experience, in the cooperation, interest, and enthusiasm which is represented by a well-selected building committee of the church, a more welcoming and fertile challenge to his ability than he finds in working with building committees of the secular fields. The committee chosen for serving in building a church is usually a committee of quite varied experiences and training. It brings that freshness and vigilance which, if allowed to mature slowly and intelligently in the process of working with the architect, can promise splendid results.

In the majority of cases, the selection of a building committee by the church precedes the selection of an architect. The architect may occasionally be chosen from among the church group itself, but more often he is chosen because of previous work which bears the approval of members of the committee. This means that he is not necessarily a member of their congregation or of their denomination.

The selection of an architect who has had experience in church building and whose work has proved successful and substantial bears a stamp of sanity, but it is not necessarily true that this is the best method. There have been many examples where skill and ability not represented by previous performance in exactly the same field have resulted in charming and excellent work.

Occasionally, the building committee, finding it difficult to arrive at a definite decision as to its architect, feels that it is best to call upon a number of architects to visit with them and to show or explain the amount of church building which they have done. We can sympathize with this view. The large responsibility of the committee, and the seriousness with which it accepts and undertakes its duties, justify ample time for examination, study, and decision.

Calling upon architects to meet with the committee and explain their understanding of church building, their preparation and experience in the field, and the results which they have attained, should be done in a very orderly manner. Considerable care should be given to the selection of the architects that will visit the committee. Personal elements, personal friendships and acquaintances, should be minimized, with the determination to place the decision entirely upon a professional basis. This is more difficult among some committees than among others. The committee members themselves, within their group, should try for their own good to proceed in a more judicial manner than they might in work

*Trinity Methodist Church, Houston, Texas. George Pierce and Abel Pierce, Architects. Photo by Bernard*

to be done for them as individual clients. They should view the architect as one who will be a co-worker with them, giving his enthusiasm and his ability in the same degree that they give their service for the good of the church.

It is important for the building committee to realize that greater requirements of a professional nature are placed upon the architect in the planning and building of a church than in nearly any other field of building activity. The need for personal time and work is unusually large at all stages. In addition, more prolonged study, much wider travel and very considerable apprenticeship have been required of the architect in preparation for practice in church building. The fees paid to the architect are correspondingly higher than those paid for commercial work. It is both fitting and necessary that the committee understand its obligations when decisions and contracts confirming the selection of the architect are made.

The building committee is usually made up of a number of members, ranging possibly from seven to nine; experience has proved that committees of this size work well. A committee of three members often leads to the work falling, in a tremendous degree, on a single member who is willing to undertake the heavy burdens of the committee. A committee of excessive numbers is usually broken down into sub-committees. This leads to confusion, difficulty of reaching decisions, and delay. Experience with small committees, normal committees and excessively large committees convinces me that the committee of seven to nine members serves the church's interest more thoroughly and retains a personal part in all of the planning and building from its inception to its completion.

Committee members are experienced, to a high degree, in actual programs and services of the church. A number of the committee members will be ardent workers in the services of the church, or the church school, familiar with its practical needs and ideals for complete planning. Other members of the committee will have experienced the financial problems and the public problems

**9**

the church has encountered. Others are consistent, reliable laymen whose church activity has not been so continuous nor so demanding as that of the groups mentioned. A committee which represents all three of these groups of church membership can render a wider, sounder, and more satisfactory service than small groups of enthusiasts with interest in a single field.

The clergy should also be represented on the committee. Committees which work separately and apart, referring back to the clergy from time to time, are incomplete. Committees which have the clergyman as their active chairman tend to be less vocative and are given to less-studied decision than committees who work under the direction of a competent layman as chairman. The ideal approach is one in which the responsibility for a decision, whether right or wrong, does not finally fall on the shoulders of one man. A group is not necessarily more conservative nor more radical than a single individual, but it will more thoroughly assimilate values which might be considered too conservative by some individuals or too radical by others, and adjudge these to the best interest of their building problem.

Instances of work done under the direction of a small committee lead me to believe that on a small committee there is usually one dominant figure willing to work, willing to take responsibility, and with practical experience in his parish. After an initial series of committee meetings, the work, from week to week, is performed by this committeeman. In the parish there are many opinions, almost as many opinions as there are members. Some of these opinions can be useful and constructive. They become known best when they can be expressed to committeemen who are members of a relatively large committee. The fact that a single individual is doing 90 per cent of the work leads to a withholding of such opinions, some of which might be very useful. It later leads to the expressing of these opinions in a cumulative manner, causing embarrassment or offense to the building committee leader. It also tends to cause delay, expense, and change in the preparation of the drawings. For this reason it should be recommended as a sensible course to choose a committee not exceeding nine and not smaller than five members, widely versed in the different activities of the church and in their professional, business, and commercial experience.

The architect, in dealing with such a committee, will find a variety of skills and outstanding experiences represented. Such a committee may include business men active in banking or manufacturing, others less active in these fields but intensely interested in the church school and leaders of it through many years, a church official familiar with its normal daily problems, a real estate man, a physician or surgeon active in the church, an insurance man, and possibly one or two men no longer active in business but with long church service. From these a diversity of views and opinions can be expected at the beginning. These opinions gradually merge themselves into some common grounds of approach, and with the leadership of an understanding, open-minded chairman tend to create a clear vision of the church's financial and idealistic possibilities, and the manner in which these should be approached, keeping first things first.

The procedure suggested in forming the building committee of the church is indeed an entirely practical one. The position of the clergy must be considered further in this respect. We have very frankly-stated opinions of the clergy in this matter. They report that in certain instances the building committee and the architect failed to understand fully the traditional values of the church and the primacy of its emotional meaning; that buildings have reflected incomplete comprehension of the religious aspects sought by the clergy. Without question, the clergy are correct in taking such a position if they have encountered such an experience. I have never worked with a building committee which proceeded without the fullest cooperation of the clergy and without repeated conferences with them. The position both of the committee and of the clergy is very much stronger because of this cooperation than it would be if either were acting alone. The architect serves in a professional and judicial capacity by which he is obligated to promote this complete understanding. Where objections have been raised by the clergy, they seem most often to have been raised because of the architect's egoism which caused him to promote solutions which were not opposed by the committee, but which failed to express the ritualistic requirements so real in the mind of the clergy.

In whatever manner the architect is chosen by the committee and approved by the authorities of the church, his work begins in interpreting the decisions made by the committee in its preliminary judgments. From these the extent of the physical plant, and the needs of its various functions can be developed. The degree to which it can or cannot pass beyond minimum structural costs will be indicated.

The next stage is to digest, analyze, and visualize the possibilities of meeting this program successfully. The architect must, as early as he possibly can, prepare a diagrammatic solution so that he may judge the volume and area of building required, and make a reasonable estimate of its approximate cost. All of these facts must be given to the committee in consultation, so that an overall picture of what is and what is not possible may be determined. It is unfortunate for the architect, and equally unfortunate for the committee, to be misled by undue enthusiasms. It is, however, important that the artistic and the completely useful planning for every function desired by the committee be made clear. If these cannot be reached within the means anticipated they may be made possible by funds contributed later.

The architect will find that if his work is convincing in the sense of structure, and clean-cut in planning, the committee will be his greatest supporters. From that stage on, beautiful but quick sketches, suggestions, even idealistic beyond what might be contemplated as essential, frequently bring recognition by a member or donor. This adds a growing interest to the common and community sense of building that will eventually make the church a possession of the congregation through a widespread, understanding cooperation in its planning and building.

Experience in the approach to church building from what we might call the opposite direction, will lead any architect to avoid it. The quick choice of a predetermined plan, the undetachable adherence to a previously-built form, crosses out from the beginning the creative challenge which the architect should welcome. No church building is necessarily like unto another in all its extent and detail. No single parish has to meet exactly the same problems that are found in another parish. The church exceeds this narrowing approach and demands an open and advancing vision from those who seek to build in this modern day with our modern methods and materials.

There is, at the beginning, a tendency for the building committee to look on the architect as a person of thorough knowledge and ability, in a position to tell them practically everything that they need to know concerning the design of their church. This opinion places the architect at a serious disadvantage. It is an opinion that he does not desire and does not merit. He cannot build a good church without the complete constructive cooperation of the committee. The sooner he makes this clear to the committee, the more thorough will be the work of both. The architect and the building committee should meet frequently. Criticisms and suggestions made by individual members should be recorded and carefully considered by the architect. These opinions often accent the particular interest of that committee member as to a portion of the building, or to work within a portion of the building, with

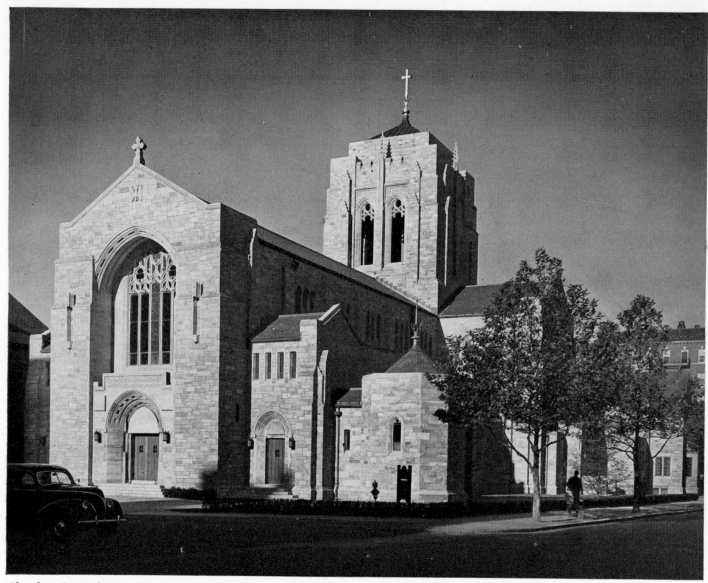

*Church of Our Lady Queen of Martyrs, Forest Hills, Long Island, New York. Maginnis and Walsh, Architects. Photo by Sigurd-Fischer*

which he is especially familiar. There may be a tendency to over-accent the space requirements in the field of his interest. Here a widely-experienced committee will coordinate and relate the particular interest to a reasonable pattern consistent with the overall limits of this church.

The opinions and suggestions are creative elements in forming the mind of the entire committee. They cause the picture to be clearer in the minds of the groups. They aid the architect in more clearly understanding the problems he is seeking to solve well. The fact that committee meetings are held frequently is an advantage to the architect in timing his progress in drawing and planning. Changes and rearrangements of plan are made at a stage when they entail relatively little waste of money and relatively little delay in the office. It avoids the inertia and resistance which develop when plans which have been formulated to a considerable degree must be readapted to further suggestions of committee members. The committee itself is more flexible under these circumstances.

Often a consulting architect, in addition to the architect, is employed by the committee on the design of a church. The distinction should be made very clear to the committee and the work of each of the architects definitely defined. While the overall pattern of the building may be suggested and outlined in reasonable detail by the consulting architect, the actual service as architect by the architect should be in no way impaired. His right to create, develop and build the building should hold all of its normal privileges. Unless this is true, the committee cannot expect the degree of enthusiasm and constant service from the architect that he would render in the absence of a consultant. Once again the imperative thing is the mutual helpful cooperation of architect, consultant and committee in reaching opinions and decisions for the good of the church. The experience of the consultant should become a stimulant for high endeavor by the architect, inviting and encouraging him to freedom in reaching beautiful results.

Throughout the stage of all preliminary planning, throughout the stage of working drawings and even preparation of specifications and details, frequent meetings with the committee are to be recommended. For this reason, the committee should be a permanent committee with as little change as possible of membership. Gradually, as the structure takes form, as the plans pass from paper to material, each member of the committee becomes more enthusiastic as a participant in this work. The building becomes his building. Cooperation often becomes even greater than it was at the beginning. The architect finds a most happy response from this personal interest and participation of the individual members.

# THE MODERN CHURCH REQUIRES AN ADEQUATE AREA

The site on which the church is to be built is usually chosen before the architect is selected. The adequacy of this site is a requirement of primary importance in planning churches for our modern cities. The consistent growth of the functions delegated to the church school shows us clearly that sites which thirty years ago were considered adequate for a good church, were in truth inadequate.

The need of building a new church is very often brought about because an inadequate old location has become more and more undesirable, losing increasing numbers of church members to more modern and convenient housing areas. This indicates that the choice of the site, in a desirable new location and in an area large enough to allow intelligent planning, must be studied by the church committee. Many of our modern church buildings have been occasioned by the migrations of populations to suburban areas, hitherto undeveloped, where a new church is a necessity for the convenience of its members.

The new churches which we are building beyond the built-up city zones are usually churches of modest requirements at the time of their initial building. However, their builders, both clergy and laymen, invariably view with optimistic anticipation the possible growth of their plant and an increase in its facilities. Consequently, the land requirements should receive intelligent study.

Assume, for example, a church plant that contemplates a nave large enough to seat in the neighborhood of 500 members. If this plant is laid out carefully to meet the needs of the church school and attendant functions as well as those of the church itself, we shall find it difficult to create an attractive modern architectural solution on an area of less than 60,000 sq. ft., approximately 200 by 300 ft.

The modern building committee takes very seriously the problem of parking space for the cars of its parishioners. The street curb boundaries will care for but a small portion of this parking requirement. Some thought must be given to providing a convenient parking lot, not too large in area, and so developed that it will not be offensive in appearance nor detract from the church grounds and buildings. Various estimates have been made as to the approximate number of cars to be cared for at any Sunday service when the church is comfortably filled. In the instance we have chosen, the church of 500, a conservative opinion would indicate that provision for approximately 100 cars would be adequate. These would not all have to be parked on the church property. Some 20 to 30 of them may be parked along the curbs for the hours of service.

Permission is usually granted for such parking, even though it is not normally allowed at other hours.

Continuing our example, and assuming that we are restricted to what we have said would be a minimum area, some 60,000 sq. ft., and that a portion of this area is to be assigned to a parking zone, we would find that one-fourth of our land is required for this purpose. It is my feeling that the provision of a completely adequate site should be of primary importance in all decisions as to the location of a new church. Even for a church of 500, we could wisely seek area approaching more nearly 80,000 sq. ft. than limit ourselves to the reasonably minimum area.

From the architect's point of view, a site with modest change of contour, gentle slopes, and blessed with splendid trees, is the ideal site. Excessive slope, while suggesting charm for picturesque arrangements, usually requires more costly construction, and is to a degree less useful than one of more modest slope. In many instances the land will be practically flat. Here the landscaping, the gardens, and the grouping of heavier shrubbery will have to substitute for a more natural beauty of the site.

The location will be most satisfactory if it is surrounded by residential development. Immediate proximity to suburban centers of business or amusement is not advantageous, although it is not necessary for great distance to separate such centers from the site chosen for the church.

The practical problem of securing such areas as we should like to have for our church determines what is possible and what is not possible. The newer, more correctly planned suburban areas usually provide blocks of greater overall dimension than was formerly true; certainly larger than those which were found within older cities. Such areas, as approximately the two acres which we have mentioned above, frequently are obtainable within reasonable cost. In suburban areas, the land cost is relatively small in proportion to the total overall cost of the church plant. Economy is unwise when it results in the choice of a small amount of land adequate only for the initial building requirements. City planners and architects representing the city encounter constantly problems of planning for the future as they deal with parks, schools, and housing developments. We must realize that the church should hold as great an importance, which should not recede when a new, permanent building is started in a new and desirable neighborhood. We have a long way to go before we can become thoroughly satisfied with the position the church occupies in our civilization.

Francis Bond in his *Introduction to Gothic Architecture in England* estimates the number of churches in England in the fourteenth century to have been one parish church for each 240 to 250 persons living in the locality. We know that those parish churches, in a great majority, were well-built stone churches, so well-built that many have remained until the present day.

Small sites typical of city churches during the past two generations led to the building of church walls and the walls of the church school very close to the lines of the church property. The lack of lawns and grass areas tended to harden and make less inviting the appearance of the entire church building. It definitely intensified the noise problem. An area of relative quiet, having little traffic during the normal hours of service, will be a great advantage to our modern church. The more charming modern designs have availed themselves of glass exposures looking out on attractive gardens. These provide quiet areas that do not detract from the service within the church. To accomplish this, the view must not include traffic on adjacent streets.

As we pursue our study of the needs of the modern church, we shall recognize the requirement for provision for enlargement or expansion at a future time.

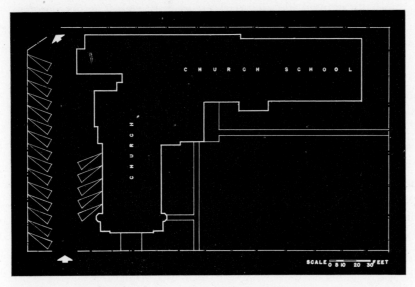

*Site Plan, St. Mark's Church,*
*Beaumont, Texas.*
*William Ward Watkin, Architect*

This has bearing on the original selection of the site. Often an existing church, serving its purposes quite well but with need for greater area, is located on a site which permits only vertical expansion, usually involving costly rebuilding to meet modern fireproof structure code requirements. As a result, the decision is made to build a new church on a more convenient site, adequate for all of its needs, and to realize as much as possible from the sale of the existing property. Where the existing site leaves reasonable excess area, careful planning can accomplish to a minimum degree, the points mentioned above. Notice, for example, the arrangement of St. Mark's Church, Beaumont, Texas, (above). The first construction on the site consisted of the church school, with the second floor of this building designed as a chapel with open-timbered ceiling. This unit was used without further building for a number of years until such a time as the church proper and additional rooms for the church school could be built. The church was grouped around an open garden. The windows of both the church school and the church were quite away from the main traffic street bordering the property. The vacant area behind the church auditorium, though not large, was developed into a parking zone. This was accomplished without detriment to the appearance of the entire church plant, and yet kept the parking area close to the building. The accompanying view of the exterior of this church (page 17) will make clear how completely the area designed for parking has been hidden away in a manner that makes it free from offense from almost any point of view.

In a number of rather large recent developments of city and suburban churches, the development of the parking area as an essential to the site plan has been poorly handled. The large areas assigned to parking have wrapped themselves around a considerable portion of the site, and have been left as bare, open zones, unpleasant in color contrast with the lawns and walls of the building. They appear visibly wasteful in their idle periods, and disfiguring in their busy periods. It is appropriate that a finer sense of planning, a more garden-like quality of landscaping and a greater consistency with a beautiful church and church school plant should be sought and achieved.

Such areas as I have suggested as minimum sites are indeed small when we compare them with sites obligatory for elementary schools. For quite a number of years good planning of schools has recommended an area of not less than six acres as minimum for an elementary school of approximately 800 pupils. Many schools have used to advantage almost twice this area. The same is true in the rapidly developing element which we call the suburban community center or shopping center. Whether this be simply the supermarket or a combination of other commercial elements with the market, the importance of areas adequate for parking automobiles at peak hours has been accepted. The architectural solution of these areas has usually been dull, and in most cases arrangement is unpleasant. Solutions of the next few years will recognize the need of finished appearance, neatness in arrangement and added artistry in place of bareness.

In considering the area required for the church site, we should remember that in modern work there is more and more of a tendency, wherever possible, to confine elements of the church school to buildings of one level. In the planning of the elementary school, the two-story solution has disappeared with greater acceptance of the one-story plan, and we can expect a similar development in church school planning. If the site is adequate there is economy in building this type of building. The grounds, gardens and courts which can be developed because of the extended nature of the one-story plan are very attractive. Therefore, wherever possible in site selection, consideration should be given to the one-story solution. If this solution is chosen, a greater amount of land will be required.

Two factors—the constant call for flexibility in modern planning, and the fact that seldom can an entire and complete scheme be built within the initial building cost—favor plans of the one-story type, which adapt themselves readily to partial initial building and later completion. Modern tendencies in the matter of height within the church itself are towards less loftiness than was considered essential a generation ago. The lofty church carries dignity which we long to achieve, yet often becomes exceedingly costly and in many cases impractical to heat and treat acoustically. The loftier height of the church itself as compared with the church school is essential. Two- or possibly three-story school groups, adjacent to a very lofty church, were not unusual in the work of the past generation. Skill in design was necessary to express the quieter and more modest function of the school and keep the greater dignity due the church. A similar consistency can be looked for in the dominance of a splendid but less lofty modern church in a group composed of the church with its one-story school. The school in this case remains close to the ground. Charming solutions of this type are beginning to appear.

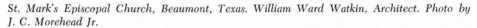

*St. Mark's Episcopal Church, Beaumont, Texas. William Ward Watkin, Architect. Photo by J. C. Morehead Jr.*

Modern forms are sometimes offensive, but seem to be progressing toward refinement that will eventually be satisfying. It is therefore appropriate that the thoughts of church builders be related to their problem when they are about to choose their new location and land necessary for its complete development.

Church building faces a field of increasing importance in these days of social unrest. As we build beautiful and noble churches, we render service that sustains our freedom and independence and advances our loyalty to our nation and our righteous leadership in the affairs of the world. Each church group which develops useful meaning, public interest, and high ideals within its congregation moves forward toward a better and safer civilization. Old as is the problem of the church, its solutions are still new for our age. The great interests that the cathedrals of the past cultured among the Christians of their day are the same building interests, creative interests and churchly interests which it is our duty to hold, and to build in our own manner and in our own day so that it, too, may be a day of Godly value.

After the site has been selected and the architect chosen, the building committee presents its requirements to the architect. These may be in the form of notes outlining the essential parts of the building and its extent. More detail or understanding of these requirements develops from day to day with the conferences between the architect and the committee. After a time these will have congealed to a reasonable program for the plant necessary for this particular church.

The period of preliminary planning—often rather lengthy—is the period in which the church gradually takes form, and becomes, at least to the architect, very much of a reality. It is at this stage that he has the opportunity to test a number of different solutions for practical value and for artistic composition and beauty. As he has to start with something definite, it is logical to start with the church plan. The architect has available a long record of historic building. Plan solutions, the arrangement of the seating in the church, the suitable dignity and space of his sanctuary, and the interesting and inviting entry forming the narthex come first. Height, width and length in their simplest but most direct sense are indicated by the extent of his program requirements.

The architect does not create by means of plan forms alone. He is constantly aware of the relations of space within his building, which are determined by height. In a much richer sense he visualizes the entire composition and its possible expression of meaning and beauty. He learns this more completely as he continues his preliminary studies.

The simple basilican plan form, with or without the lower aisle sections, is understood by clergy and laymen, and becomes clearer to them as the architect's schemes take initial form. If the architect intends to arrange his seating in a new or novel manner, it is more difficult for him to present clearly in the initial stages his idea of the entire interior composition; its height, width and form.

The manner in which the architect approaches his first preliminary studies and the plan forms will vary. I can recall the manner of Cram—a most unusual one. On a sheet of Whatman's paper he would draw in ink the outline of a pier, the spacing pier to pier, and the center points and stilt of his arch, often using both green and red ink on the same diagram. The number of piers would be indicated; usually four or five would set up the dimensions of a modest nave. The line of the inner face of the wall of the sanctuary and its

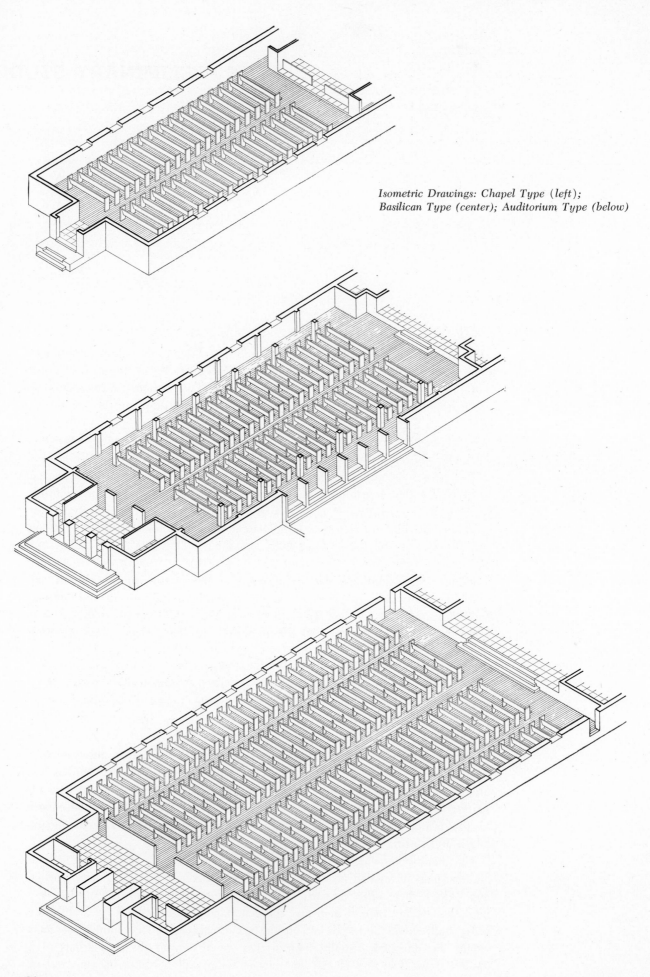

*Isometric Drawings: Chapel Type (left);*
*Basilican Type (center); Auditorium Type (below)*

shape would be drawn. The height of the truss of the nave and the type of its members would be quite clear. This and this alone constituted the starting point for a church. Familiarity with thousands of plans of the past made it possible for him to visualize his design and its composition and to determine it in this simple manner. This approach presupposed that the draftsman had first-hand acquaintance with many English parish churches, gained by considerable travel and study. Planning of the exterior and of such additional parts as the smaller church school of his day, were left for development as the drawings progressed. This was a hard and rigid manner because it predetermined the entire form, and, in a sense, limited the development and the more sensitive fitness of the entire scheme.

Nothing can be more inappropriate than to start the preliminary work for a modest parish church from the plan forms of vast churches. Too often in recent generations, many inappropriate forms, having no rightful place in the parish church, were built as historic reminders suitable only to great churches.

The practice of each individual architect varies at the stage of preliminary drawings, but in the majority of cases a man seeks to visualize his plan form as a complete building, and thinks in terms of the entire perspective mass which the plant will require. Often some very happy solutions are indicated at this early stage which have such merit that they persist in dominating further planning. If pursued with constant study, this may prove to be an excellent method. Usually, however, the plan forms are worked out first in considerable detail as to exact arrangement and areas for all portions of the plant.

Starting with our preliminary designs of the church, we will want to know, approximately, whether our building appropriation is sufficient to cover the minimum requirements of the plant, or, in other words, how extensive a building we can have.

The number of seatings to be provided has been definitely determined by the committee in consultation with the architect. At least this has been determined within a modest range of variance not exceeding some 10 or 15 per cent. From this number of seatings we devise an arrangement of the pews and the aisles, likewise set up the required length and width within the nave. There will be several suitable arrangements which have proved satisfactory elsewhere. We may make other less traditional arrangements, or at least experiment with them for our own information.

In practically every case there is a valid reason for a central aisle leading from the church entrance to the sanctuary. Only occasionally have plan forms which abandon the central aisle been appropriate, and then under very unusual circumstances.

With the seating divided equally to the right and to the left of the central aisle in a symmetrical arrangement extending throughout the nave, we produce the simplest type of plan form. For convenience, we will call this the chapel form (page 20). With pews seating not more than 10 persons per pew, or 20 persons for the width of the church, the plan form provides a central aisle and an aisle to the right and left following the contour of the outer walls. Such a plan would immediately determine the length of the nave. The committee's program will have determined the required seating capacity. This in turn will determine the number of pews required in the chapel plan, and therefore the length of the nave. Testing our dimensions will make it apparent whether we are within safe bounds or exceeding them. We would prefer to have no pew farther than 110 ft. from the chancel. If our seating requirements indicate that this length will be exceeded, we will test plan arrangements using greater width, either with the pews occupying the width of the nave and aisles of basilican type beyond them, or, if necessary, with additional rows of pews to the right and left of the side aisles. In each case we will test for our overall width and our overall length with the idea of reaching proportions which will be both attractive and valid for use.

We will find that width is the most difficult dimension. As width is increased by the required number of seatings, we must add greater height. The simplest and most satisfactory plans under these conditions will not require us to place seatings on the outer aisles (page 20). Such plans are usually developed in what we will term the basilican type of plan.

The traditional church plan, even in parish churches of relatively small seating requirements, often placed the piers supporting the clerestory between the nave and the aisles. This was an attractive form offering beauty of architectural treatment, and held high acceptance on the part of the laymen, provided the aisle space remained aisle space and did not become seating space.

If our testing for arrangements appropriate to the required seatings proves that even the basilican type must extend to greater length than we desire, we will have to try the auditorium type (page 20). In this arrangement, additional seatings will be placed beyond the side aisles. We know that we do not want these additional seatings separated from the nave by piers of the basilican type, because of the unpleasant separation of the congregation seated in these areas. With the auditorium type we will be called upon to study our proportions and our ceiling heights carefully in order to retain an attractive form. It is easy for an interior of the auditorium type to become dull and uninteresting.

There is no reason why we should not invite the fullest freedom of the artistry of our architects to create new and improved plans and buildings, provided that such plans are consistent with the dignity and noble meaning of the church. In this respect the architect should recognize and hold constantly in mind that he must know thoroughly the practices and traditions of the church which he is to build, in order that his creation may become a true and beautiful expression of those high practices and traditions. He should under no circumstance treat the church as a guinea pig for his own personal experimentation in new and novel forms unrelated to religious expression and possibly offensive to churchmen.

A charmingly direct yet entirely modern arrangement appears in the plan of the First Methodist Church of Midland, Michigan (page 23) for which Alden Dow was the architect. The plan holds to the chapel form, with central aisle and aisles to the right and left. Courts and gardens flank both sides of the nave. The chapel is advanced to the front of the church, and reached by means of the church vestibule. It is balanced on the opposite side by the ladies' lounge. The nursery, kindergarten and infant section of the church school are placed on the main floor level, with the major portion of the church school occupying area at a level below the main floor.

A survey of the seating capacities indicated in plans of recent churches shows an average range between 400 and 450 persons. A number of smaller churches, or chapels, are still built for requirements of between 250 and 300 persons. Many more churches exceed the 450 seatings and pass to numbers ranging from 600 to 1000. With nearly all of these church forms or plans, from the average level up to the very large churches, one or more chapels seating from 40 to as large a number as 120 persons are appropriate according to the capacity of the church. These chapels are being equipped to serve well on festival days when the church attendance exceeds capacity. However, the privacy and charm of the chapel are retained in the best examples. It serves to the best advantage when it is not directly open into the area of the church, but has a sensitive separation and intimacy of treatment.

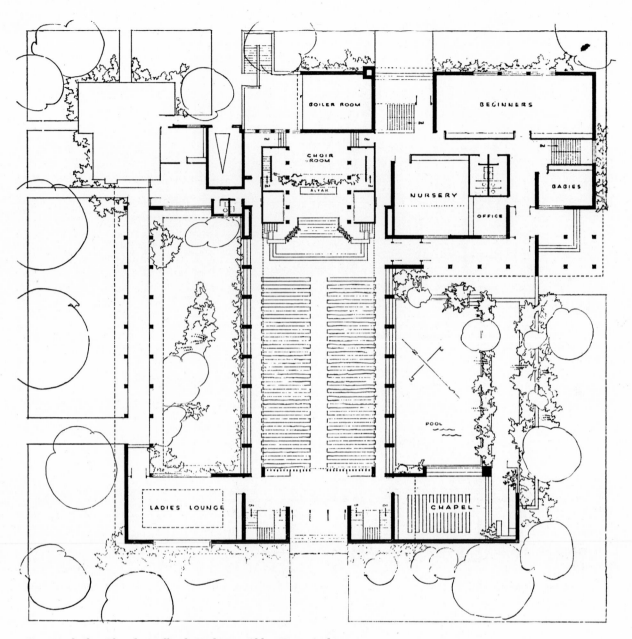

BOILER ROOM

BEGINNERS

CHOIR ROOM

NURSERY

BABIES

ALTAR

OFFICE

POOL

LADIES LOUNGE

CHAPEL

*First Methodist Church, Midland, Michigan. Alden Dow, Architect*

The chapel should, if possible, be so located that it can be easily reached without entering either the church or the church school. The chapel represents an element of the plan which we might call individual and personal. It affords a refuge for prayer and meditation to which members go throughout the day as individuals and not as participants in a service. Convenience and welcoming location are therefore important in the development of the plan.

A very splendid solution of the type which confines the major portion of the seating to the nave itself, is found in the plan of St. Thomas' Church in New York, as designed by Cram, Goodhue and Ferguson. As we enter the church and proceed toward the sanctuary, we find that the aisle to the left is widened for a considerable distance to care for additional seatings facing the chapel at the end of the aisle. Similar plans, with the aisle widened only as it nears the sanctuary, or with the chapel on one or both sides, have been developed and were excellent when built.

In churches of such dimensions as to demand a wider nave throughout the

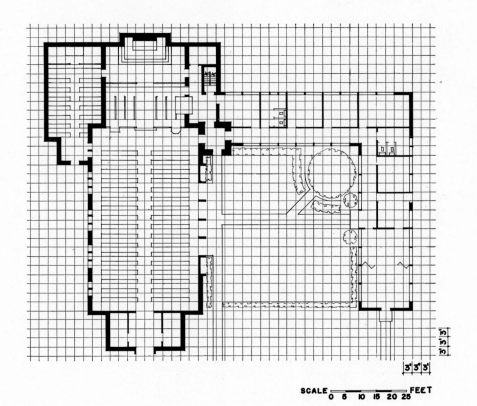

*Modular Plans:*
*Chapel Type (left);*
*Basilican Type (below*

SCALE 0 5 10 15 20 25 FEET

3' 3' 3'

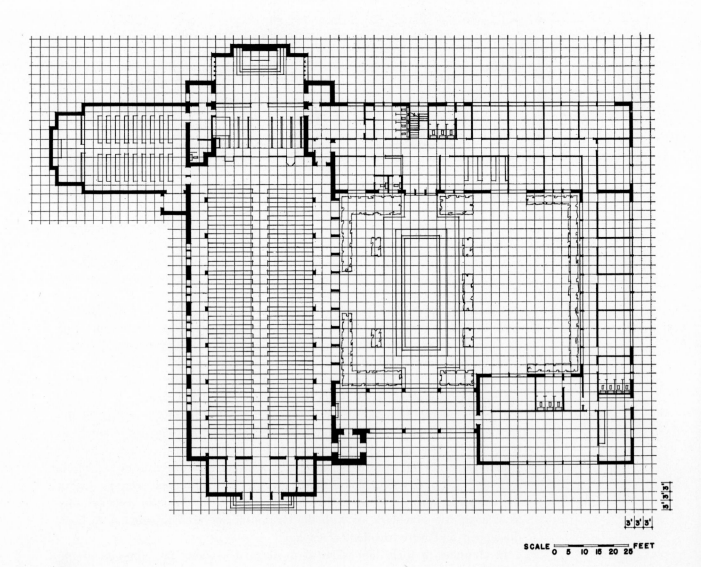

3' 3' 3'

SCALE 0 5 10 15 20 25 FEET

entire length, the architect will serve best if he devotes his skill to providing wider space free from any piers separating the central area from the aisles. He will have more nearly an auditorium type of area to deal with than in traditional forms; nevertheless many such plans have been solved well and with beauty.

Among the more modern churches, plans or studies in preliminary form have placed the pews unevenly around a central aisle which is not actually on center with the nave. Congregations would develop their own enthusiasm or disfavor from experience with this type of plan. It appears to be unfortunate, and an unusual and possibly inconvenient arrangement will be necessary to cause the sanctuary to appear in proper conformity to the seating.

The practice of preparing a program which will accompany the preliminary drawings or models deserves very favorable consideration. This program prepared by the architect reflects his understanding of the requirements of the building as developed in his meetings with the committees or authorities of the church. Such a program would place as its principal requirements the number of seatings for which the church is to be planned, the approximate area of the sanctuary, the number of persons in the choir, the approximate area of the narthex, the number of sacristies, the offices of the clergy, the number and size of classrooms and assembly rooms and any special rooms.

From programs prepared by Prof. Joseph Murphy of St. Louis in connection with his churches, we find certain constants which are of primary importance. For example:

An important requirement is that a strict economy be expressed in the planning of the building in order that it may be constructed within the most reasonable possible cost commensurate with dignity, durability, and comfort. The altar is the heart of the church. The sanctuary which shelters the altar is next in importance. The nave which shelters the congregation is next in order, and so on through the several related elements of the church.

A program along which the architect's work may be charted for orderly procedure works well if carried out in the following manner:

After the architect has met with the building committee and the clergy and an approximate "meeting of the minds" has been reached, the first step should be to examine the site. If the site has not been chosen, the first step will be to aid the committee in making a good selection. On visiting the site the architect will follow his usual procedure. He will evaluate its natural advantages, appraise the approximate avenues of approach, and consider secondary service approaches, provisions for drainage, and the general overall picture of appropriate massing and placing of the building on that particular site.

If the church is being planned for an existing congregation which is now moving to a new location, a series of careful tables should be made covering attendance records. For the church school, a weekly report at each class level including the adult levels is usually available and can be put into very accurate form with the help of the secretary of the church. A similar record should be made of attendance at church services, and accommodations in the old church should be examined to determine in what respects they were used to capacity or were over-crowded, and in what respects they were seldom used. To this data must be added, on the advice of the clergy and the building committee, what membership potential is to be expected in the new location. Does this anticipate a steady but moderate growth, or does it invite unusual growth? How shall plans be made to meet the growth anticipated?

If the former church was in a down-town location, the records will probably show rather heavy attendance at the adult level, close to or beyond the capacity of the old church. These records will also show low attendance at the primary level, and often will show that that attendance has been decreasing rather than increasing for a number of years. While a condition of this sort is normal to old churches located inconveniently for parking and distant from the majority of their members, it is not a condition to be anticipated in the new church. In the new church the primary levels and intermediate levels will immediately show much improved attendance.

From the data so secured and agreed upon as valid by the clergy and the building committee, the architect should lay out a general plan which will provide for a church and a church school adequate for the immediate needs and for normal growth for some years to come. The general plan will be a schematic diagram showing the position of the buildings on the site. The church architect whose interest is high in his work will very likely try two, three or four such schematic diagrams, and consider the merits and demerits of one against another. It is not good practice to make too many such diagrams, since this will lead to confusion. It is often excellent practice to present at least two schematic diagrams to the committee, and to go over in detail with them the points of merit and possible demerit in each scheme. Degrees of experience on the part of the committee members will be reflected in the opinions expressed, and the final general plan (or master plan as it is sometimes called) will evolve from these meetings.

Under normal conditions the architect develops such schematic diagrams within a period ranging from two weeks to a month. This period, if undue delay is avoided, can be followed by developed schematic diagrams reflecting the opinions and decisions of the architect and the committee. This work usually takes approximately three meetings, and from two to three weeks of actual elapsed time. The result of these first activities will be to establish a general plan, portions or all of which are to be built as promptly as the drawings can be developed and the work begun. The major requirement is that there should be a general plan, and all work in the initial construction should conform to it.

As we have mentioned in connection with the programs prepared by Professor Murphy, it is well to outline short but written records of the extent of facilities to be provided under this master plan: the number of seatings in the church, the number of seatings in the chapel, the size of the choir, the approximate area of the sanctuary, the number of assembly rooms in the school, the number of classrooms in the school, the extent of the nursery and primary department, the number of rooms of special purpose, the area for administrative offices, the principal building materials to be used, etc. The architect and the committee should not be handicapped by lengthy description of these elements, nor, on the other hand, should the program be an abbreviated specification. It should simply present a clear picture of the object to be accomplished.

The record should be sure to show the intent of adequate church school facilities, and include the definite meaning of the areas. This is important. Donors have a habit of giving for the church and restricting or limiting themselves for the church school. All facilities of the general plan are of such importance that their need should be a matter of record.

Continuing our survey of the architect's preliminary studies, we find an advantage in a more regular system of planning. In modern work this is spoken of as a grid, or the acceptance of regular rather than irregular spacing of supports and of many of the elements of structure. If by means of a grid we can develop methods which lead to intelligent building and intelligent use of modern materials and methods of workmanship, we should be willing to test it and to use it in planning our churches.

A grid of 3-ft. spacing seems ideally adapted for the church. Since 3-ft.

spacing is normal for pews, it is suitable to employ a grid whose multiples are repeats of this dimension. In the accompanying diagrams such schematic plans are shown.

For purpose of reading these diagrams easily, we shall begin at the entrance of the church. Here, some 12 or 15 ft. provide for the narthex vestibule. Within the church from the wall of the narthex to the front of the chancel, multiples of 3 ft. work perfectly. Where many seatings are required, two modules (or 6 ft.) provide comfortable and useful circulation for the aisle behind the last pew. Pew spaces at 3 ft. each, according to the number required, carry our module unit to the front of the first pew nearest to the chancel. Three modules (9 ft.), or four modules (12 ft.), should be assigned from first pew to the face of the chancel.

Correspondingly, a 3-ft. module is appropriate for our width in the nave. Assuming normal numbers or capacities, widths of 30 ft. (or ten modules), 33 ft. (or eleven modules), and 36 ft. (or twelve modules), are desirable for the church's 300 seatings, 400 seatings, or 500 seatings, respectively. The 36-ft. width provides 20 seatings per row of pews. The 33-ft. width provides 18 seatings per row of pews and the 30-ft. width provides 16 seatings per row of pews. Corresponding diminutions or increases in the number of modules provide for either smaller or larger numbers of seatings.

Whether the plan form be the basilican form or the chapel form, the workability of the grid is not affected. One module (or 3 ft.) will serve for the aisle near the wall in the chapel type. Two modules (or 6 ft.) will serve very attractively for the piers and the circulation aisle near the wall in the basilican type.

*First Baptist Church, Longview, Texas.*
*Wilson, Morris and Crain, Architects*

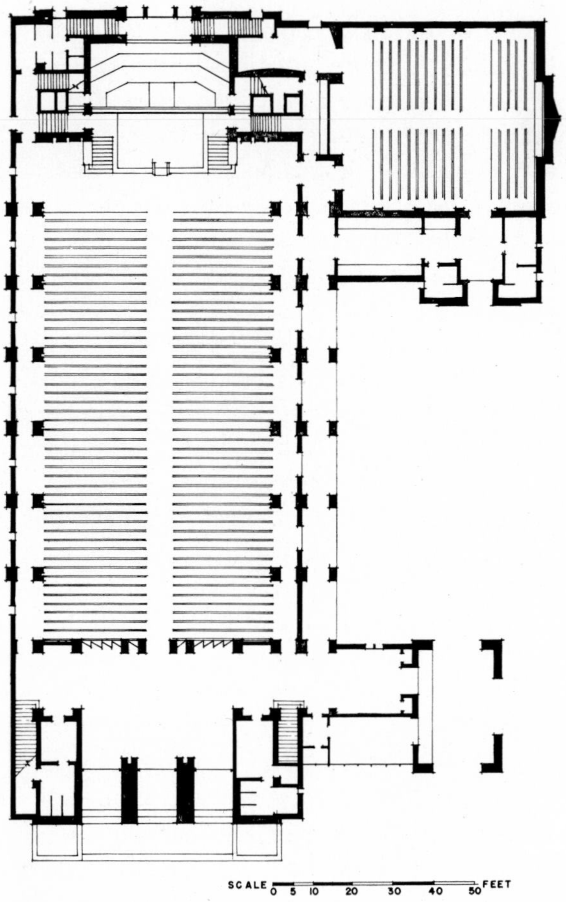

SCALE 0 5 10 20 30 40 50 FEET

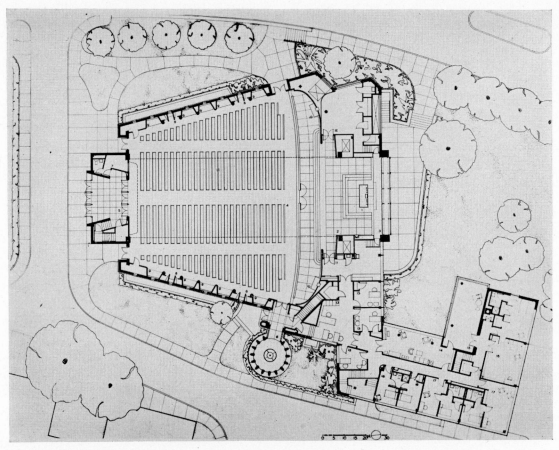

*St. Ann's Church, Normandy, Missouri. Joseph Murphy, Architect*

One of the most common and unpleasant practices in traditional work was its failure to relate intelligently the spacing of piers to the required spacing of pews. Because a pier with the arch above it seemed very beautiful when drawn in this manner or that manner to reach a proportion which appealed to the architect, it was accepted and used. The fact that it missed true pew spacing by a foot or more for each pier distance, and so repeated a series of irregularities and non-conformities, was ignored. It made access to the pews from the wall aisle inconvenient and sometimes impossible in one out of every four or five pew spaces. The modular or grid type of plan corrects this immediately. Spacings 9, 12, or 15 ft. for piers, according to the designer's proposed treatment of these supporting units, work perfectly. His main effort must be to arrange the total overall number of modules or grid spacings from chancel to narthex wall so that they conform to a pattern which will permit the regular spacing of the supporting piers.

The unit carries with equal advantage into the chancel or sanctuary space. It adapts itself to the widths required as well as the depths required in these spaces, and it becomes a simple unit to carry throughout the plan of the church school plant where it is possible for us to have classrooms as small as 9 ft. or 3 modules, and of any greater size, 12 ft., 15 ft., 18 ft., etc. Change of partitions in classroom or school zones is frequent. Regular spacing is really a great advantage, since the module adapts itself to windows and other structural and material dimensions.

For purposes of convenience, the module has been used as conforming to the inside dimensions or the inner face of the exterior walls. Modular walls in units of a 4-in. dimension, usually spoken of as a module in construction, develop naturally from a 3-ft. grid, and should be accompanied by a modular wall; that is, one whose dimension is either 12 in., 16 in., 20 in., or possibly in some cases 24 in. in thickness from inner face to outer face.

Church design will not suffer because of an orderly intelligent regularity conforming with good modern building practice. The degree to which this more efficient system produces measurable economies cannot be stated in actual percentages of cost. However, sufficient work has been done to show that there is economy in such a process. This should be particularly true in church building, where architects and churchmen have been given to romanticisms in dealing with figures and dimensions which cause simple buildings to become difficult. Workmanship cannot be efficient under such circumstances. If these romanticisms really produced greatness, possibly we would be willing to pay for them, but the tendency has been for them to produce considerable confusion inappropriate to the church.

If we recall its long history of more than fifteen centuries, it is apparent how the practice of church building became an orderly practice, constantly evolving a degree of exactness. Vaulted structure could be built, and was built occasionally, in irregular and unmathematical spacings. However, the great work of any period—of the Romanesque, of the Gothic, or of the Renaissance—sought a very regular spacing of piers so that the vaults developing upon these piers and supported by them could become beautiful and mathematically perfect solutions of vaulted structure. We therefore are not making a deliberate suggestion for a change or what might be called a modern innovation. We are actually recalling the fineness of the great architectures of the past.

It is amazing to what extent the traditional basilican form repeats itself in our most modern work. The beauty of the historic stone piers and arches separating the nave from the aisle was very real, and was desirable except where it led to the placing of pews in the aisle space. The additional number of seats provided in this manner seldom served satisfactorily. The sight lines were very difficult, and persons seated in the aisle seemed separated from the richness of the service in the sanctuary. When the modern architect has chosen the basilican form without seating in the aisle space, the results have been good, just as such arrangements were good when built in either Gothic or Romanesque form. The basilican type affords an opportunity for greater height in the nave and sanctuary, with lesser

*Interior of St. Ann's Church, Normandy, Missouri. Joseph Murphy, Architect*

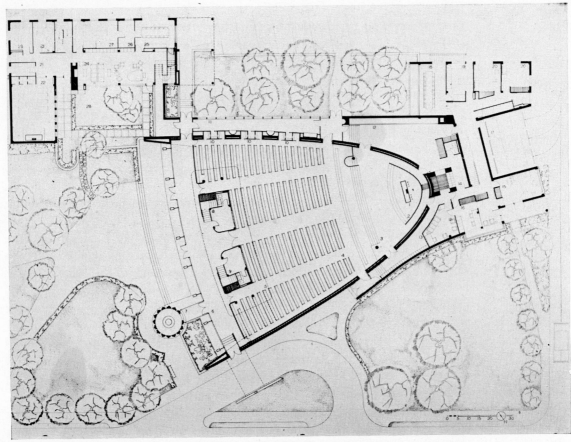

*Church of the Resurrection, St. Louis, Missouri. Joseph Murphy, Architect*

height over the circulation aisles to the right and to the left. This plan gives the modern designer opportunity for interesting composition. It is likely to be free from arches, to have lighter supporting members in place of heavy stone piers, and to have an appropriate openness of the aisles, at least on one side, to bring in vistas of gardens or other attractive settings (page 27).

The simple basilican form of modest extent was beautiful when used for the churches of Ravenna. It continued beautiful in the forms used by Sir Christopher Wren many centuries later and came to still greater favor in the churches of New England in the eighteenth century. Such long-continued acceptance by Christian civilizations surely indicated a degree of fitness. It seems logical that the more modern churches should reflect an understanding of the qualities of such a plan and should be able to give to it still greater and more timely beauty.

The consistency with which history seems to repeat itself even in the work of our most modern architects, reminds me of a position taken by Benedetto Croce in the *Breviary of Aesthetic.** He said,

A system is like a house, which as soon as it has been built and decorated has need of continuous labor, more or less energetic in order to keep it in repair, and at a certain moment there is no longer any use in restoring and propping up the system. We must demolish and reconstruct it. But with this capital difference: in the work of thought the perpetually new house is perpetually maintained by the old one, which persists in it almost by an act of magic.

A unique plan has been developed in the new Church of St. Ann now being built in St. Louis, Missouri; Joseph Murphy, architect (plan, page 28). Here the nave is not of excessive length but has unusual width. The seatings are

* *Book of the Opening of The Rice Institute*, page 432.

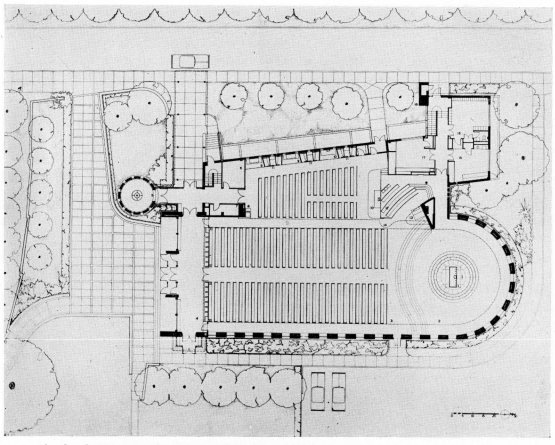

*St. Peter's Church, St. Louis, Missouri. Joseph Murphy, Architect*

shown to the right and to the left of the outer aisles. The church is planned so that it widens out as we approach the sanctuary (page 29). Fine openness is gained by this wide approach. What we might normally expect from such a plan form—that is, a rather dull interior for the nave proper—is shown in the studies as essentially the traditional cross-section of the basilican church. By continuing the lofty nave as a rectangular form throughout the entire length of the church and giving even greater height to it as it reaches the sanctuary, a dominating reality like that of a basilican church is given to the central area. To the right and to the left of this central space the ceilings over the outer seatings are lower, rather in the manner of an aisle, but without supporting piers separating the nave from the aisle. By this means complete visibility is assured for all of the congregation. The widening of the church as one approaches the sanctuary is to be commended. The frequently seen form of auditorium or amusement-hall widening toward the rear would be inappropriate for the church. In the plan which Professor Murphy has suggested, a richness of the main sanctuary and of the smaller sanctuaries of the chapels forms an inspiring perspective as one enters the church. Greater width has created greater interest. Further studies along lines indicated by this study may become very popular. In fact Professor Murphy has already developed in his proposed St. Peter's Church of St. Louis (above) a modification which provides a very clean, impressive nave form, with additional area placed at one side of the plan only.

He has also developed studies for the Church of the Resurrection (page 30), which adapt the widened seating area to a less traditional plan form, developed from the parabolic contours of the interior. In this particular plan the glazed narthex is screened, as viewed from the sanctuary, by an interesting treatment on higher levels, of the choir enclosures, which form a screen against the brilliance of glass enclosing the front of the church. In the plans of both of the churches just referred to, attractive solutions of the baptistry present a further freshness in modern planning.

Where the number of persons to be seated is unusually large, there is a tendency for building committees to consider the balcony as a possible solution. It is never a solution. It is neither convenient nor useful as compared with correct seating at the main floor level. It usually creates an unsightly interior. It adds to the problem of acoustics, and most of all to the problems of administration and of maintaining dignity of service.

The use of a limited gallery or balcony level at the rear of the church for purposes of the choir has been thoroughly satisfactory in those churches whose services require this location for the choir. Except where such a service is to be rendered, balconies or galleries designed to reduce areas within the central mass of the church and to divide its seatings at two levels should be avoided wherever possible.

Where the requirements of seating are very large, (in churches seating from 1000 to 1200 or more), the wider nave becomes a necessity. This may require a width as great as 56 to 64 ft. and a length from face of chancel steps to narthex vestibule of approximately 120 ft. Usually in these cases, the nave is treated as an auditorium type and the basilican form is avoided. Such width seems to limit the height, and certainly does if we consider the proportion of the width to the height of the room. This plan makes it difficult to plan for proper accent and direction, centering on the altar or baptistry in the sanctuary. The solution suggested for St. Ann's Church, St. Louis, widening the nave as it approaches the chancel, yet retaining a lofty central ceiling throughout the length of the nave in almost traditional manner, indicates one appropriate treatment for such large areas.

These suggestions leading to preliminary study are written of the more normal field—churches of average size and requirements. We should hope that churches of great dimension, possibly approaching cathedral magnitude, will more frequently rather than less frequently become the opportunities of our architects. From skill and sensitive power to create beauty fitting to the church of moderate dimension will develop the skills and richness of imagination required for churches of greater dimension. With all the funds at his disposal which will be necessary for such building, the architect should place his accent on true dignity and religious emotion. Such buildings will challenge our architects to reach inspiration comparable to that of the great works of the past. Our buildings should have likeness in all true religious meaning to that of the great cathedrals, but they also should be the greatest work of our time, not imitative of works of the past.

# MATERIALS FOR CHURCH CONSTRUCTION

Of what materials shall we construct our church?

We should reach our decision while the preliminary studies are in course of preparation. These preliminary studies will be far more convincing if the choice of material has been made. Fine creative design can be done only with full knowledge and awareness of the qualities of the materials from which the building will be built. There is a quality of stone; there is a quality of brick; there is a quality of concrete; and there are qualities of both steel and wood. Certainly the patterns of our church must develop according to the characteristic qualities of the materials from which it is to be erected.

I know nothing that could be more unfortunate in the planning of a church than for the architect to have designed it as a building of stone—with detail openings, walls, and towers, appropriate to stone—only to discover that his committee had decided in favor of walls of brick. The church designed originally for brick might have been even more beautiful than the one designed for stone, but two materials cannot be interchanged without great loss of beauty.

Possibly, since we are speaking of the more normal or moderate-sized church building rather than of churches of great magnitude or of cathedral scale, we shall find our first interest in the qualities of a church designed in brick. The brick walls in our churches are composed of small units which may be had in a rather wide range of color. The smaller unit of brickwork which has been general in American buildings is giving way, at least in part, to a larger dimension substituting 12 in. of length for the former 8 in. of length. The larger brick is approximately 3 in. thick, as compared with the former 2¼ in. In either dimension, bricks make an attractive wall. They are simple, do not declare themselves in a self-conscious way, and fit well in locations of residential character.

The color range of brick is perhaps its greatest disadvantage. An unfortunate choice of color has occurred too frequently in church building, with unpleasant results. The darker reds and purples, while appropriate to Georgian traditional buildings, are seldom satisfactory in open, quiet, residential neighborhoods. They may be used in the closely-built city or metropolitan areas where soot and dirt stain lighter walls so quickly.

Very light tones of brick—light grey, white, or even a pale, misty tan—defeat the architect when he tries to use them with charm and beauty for church building. The middle ranges, the soft grey-pink colors, are the most popular, and usually the most attractive. Many sections of our country have a reasonable choice of brick within these middle ranges. One can judge best what brick

*Christ Evangelical Church, Minneapolis, Minnesota. Saarinen, Saarinen & Associates, Architects. Photo by George Ryan Studios*

should be used by visiting many buildings in the city or town where the church is to be built. Viewing these buildings under different conditions of light and shadow makes it possible to choose a brick of pleasant color which will be rich enough, strong enough, and beautiful enough to make our church at home among the buildings of its environment. Bricks cannot be chosen from an individual sample or even from several samples. They must be chosen after they have been viewed in light and shade in sample walls of considerable area, surrounded by appropriate building forms, doors, and roofs to make the setting complete.

Either the usual size of brick or the larger size may be used to advantage. Perhaps the larger brick makes the walls seem stronger and the scale of the church more in keeping. There is an economy in its use, although the economy alone is not sufficient grounds to justify decision. Principally, the larger dimensions seem more interesting, and both the pattern of brickwork which results and the jointing used tend to differ from traditional old bonds. One would

*Calder Baptist Church, Beaumont, Texas. Wirtz, Calhoun and Tungate, Architects.*
*Photo by Drew*

expect designers of modern work to take advantage of this opportunity for artistry in modern design.

Of the churches now being erected, and a great many for which preliminary plans and studies are being prepared, the majority are planned with exterior walls of brick. Brick is widely accepted as a material appropriate to modern design. Its use seems equally popular with architects and laymen, and in both severely modern design and less severe modern adaptations of traditional design. The new Christ Evangelical Lutheran Church of Minneapolis (which is the work of Saarinen, Saarinen, and Associates) presents a clean-cut study of excellent brick work (page 34), beautifully handled in combination with fields of stone. On the other hand, the new Chapel for the Calder Baptist Church of Beaumont, Texas (Wirtz, Calhoun, and Tungate, Architects) presents a very interesting brick design which is both welcoming and attractive though rather conventional in form (above).

*Princeton Chapel, Princeton, New Jersey.  Cram and Ferguson, Architects.  Photo by Sigurd-Fischer*

Besides brick, the major materials in masonry are cut stone and concrete.

Stone has been the material of the traditional religious buildings throughout nearly all of church history.  Cut stone gives the walls a rich, enduring dignity. When used with artistry and skill, it is the most beautiful material we can choose.

A very beautiful example of stone work used with great artistry, yet retaining amazing simplicity within the field of traditional architecture, is to be found in the chapel at Princeton University (above) designed by Cram and Ferguson. There is an expressive clarity gained by use of contrasting fields of stone work throughout the buttresses and wall area, as compared with the good detail of the entrance, and of the West Window above the entrance. Such work justifies our longing to build masonry of well-chosen stone.

If stone is used without full appreciation of its possibilities, it can seem cold, hard, and unnecessarily sharp.  This is particularly true in the more open settings which we visualize for our modern church, and where the church is thrown into severe contrast with the buildings of residential character around it. In such locations carefully built walls of thin, split stone in grey tones, like that found in the Germantown district of Pennsylvania, would seem more inviting than regularly coursed masonry of limestone or granite. This same regularly coursed masonry, however, is entirely fitting and to be expected if we are building churches of stone in a metropolitan area where it will stand adjacent to large, towering masonry buildings.

Stone tempts the designer to turn toward tradition or toward self-conscious declaration in the degree of detail and carving wrought in its cutting. When we are dealing with stone it is more difficult to stay within reasonable bounds and to avoid excessive form. It takes great skill to limit the sculptured area to exactly the spot where it belongs, so that it will enrich the building, and not offend as excessive form or over-ornamentation.

Stone walls cost more than brick walls. If we are to build our church of cut stone we will need more money. Consequently, as stone is used in modern church building, it suggests further simplification which we may welcome, provided we emphasize strength with simplicity; quiet with all the desirable attributes that quiet gives. The stonework of the church should never be designed for display. It should be designed for sturdiness and serenity.

With this understanding of the use of stone, we find a very fine church, outstanding in its soundness and simplicity, in the Church of Our Lady Queen of Martyrs in Forest Hills, Long Island, by Maginnis and Walsh (page 39). The stone walls and tower are clean and sturdy. The stone field reflects a knowledge of good design in stonework. The skills of workmanship are far more vital than the skills of ornament. One would feel that the residents of the community, who pass this church each day, have a sense of delight in the security of religion expressed by a building of such beautiful structural form. The impression made is to be intensified, if, on passing through the portals of the church, one enters a welcoming richness of good color and ornament which fulfill the emotions of the church builder.

Concrete has at times been used successfully in church building, but it has had less popular acceptance than either brick or stone. Possibly this has been due to the association of concrete with the industrial, commercial, and utilitarian type of building rather than with the building of permanent memorial or public character. In some climates this position could be justified by the fact that after the concrete building has been erected for a few years, it appears soiled and unsightly. Our church builders would not tolerate such surface deterioration. Yet it is my opinion that we may expect still further scientific and structural quality to be developed in the use of concrete which will clearly place it on an equal footing with either brick or stone.

During the generations from the Civil War until after 1900, migrations of population from the cities and states of the East, westward, throughout the Middle West and on to the Pacific, caused many temporary wooden churches to be built. There had been charming, graceful, wooden churches built in the early days of New England. However, the wooden churches of the intervening generations had little or no likeness to a church, and certainly none of the charm of the New England chapel.

Where the church is of chapel dimension, wood is a suitable if not a lasting material. The degree of economy developed by use of wood rather than masonry, where we are forced to rigid economy, is not so great as might be imagined. Even though a chapel be charmingly done, with good taste and excellent proportion, there is the sense of the temporary rather than the permanent. Modern construction together with modern materials, and, if we are within city areas, the advanced means of fire protection, have reduced the hazard which we used to associate with buildings of wood. In this sense, the wooden church may last a long time. I doubt that it will become traditional, and I doubt that it will embody the emotional qualities which become part of the true endowment of the church. Committees might well consider that these qualities of human emotion, passing with greater richness from generation to generation, become part of the real religious meaning and the emotional stimulus of the church.

What can we say concerning steel and metals for church building? Steel is an excellent structural material. It is used in church building in much the same way it is used in commercial buildings—for columns, beams, girders, roof trusses, and the like. However, the term "steel and metal," as I am using it, suggests to me a building that may be developed out of newer and more novel materials which modern science and manufacture are developing from month to month. It will take time to become acquainted with the properties and qualities of these materials in practical use. Possibly we should call them skin materials, coverings over a structural frame, which may be of aluminum, or alloys of steel, or even of the plastics.

The practical use of these coverings in a relatively thin, well-insulated wall has been demonstrated in commercial work. It will be a matter of taste and skill in architectural design to find just how they may be used to reach the qualities required in church building.

These references have applied to material as it appears on the exterior of the church. One very large visible area which must be considered as materials are being selected is the roof. In the majority of churches, this remains a visible roof of relatively steep pitch. Therefore, its color and texture play a large part in the total color composition of the church plant. It cannot be ignored as either unimportant or immaterial.

Metals, slate, and tile are the materials normally available for the church roofing. Extreme modern forms in which the roof is practically flat, scarcely visible at all in the exterior composition, have added commercial built-up roofing materials to the list.

Either slate or metal has been used in the majority of instances. The heavily-ribbed metal roof is one of the most attractive that we can choose for a steep-pitched church roof. It seems strange it has not been more generally used. By heavily-ribbed, I mean a roof consisting of ribs built around either 2 by 2 in. wooden strips or metal forms running from the eaves to the ridge. These ribs, spaced approximately 22 in. on centers, make the most economical use of the material. The metal carries from rib to rib with an interlocking strip of metal forming a cover over the rib. This cover strip may be molded to create further interest if the architect desires. Metal roofs have in my experience shown a great deal less expense in annual upkeep than either slate or tile. The metals normally used are copper, lead, or heavy galvanized iron. The lead or the copper roofs take their color by gradual weathering. The galvanized iron must be painted to achieve the desired color, and to protect the metal against rusting.

Slate has long been the most generally used material for the roofing of our churches. In the plain black or black-grey shades, it seems rather heavy, dull and uninteresting. With the lighter shades, with considerable green or variegated tones, greater interest can be held, and the roof seems to rest appropriately for both color and weight upon the masonry walls.

Tile is seldom used except for roofs of relatively low pitch, that is, from possibly 4 to 6 in. to the foot and with buildings whose tradition is more Mediterranean than North-European. It is suitable in climates rich in sunlight. Its cost of repair and replacement is at least as great as that of slate; possibly greater.

*Church of Our Lady of Martyrs, Forest Hills, Long Island, New York. Maginnis and Walsh, Architects. Photo by Sigurd-Fischer*

Where the low-pitched roofs or the nearly-flat roof have been used in churches of modern design, the choice of built-up roofing has been unfortunate. I recall instances of very recent work in which, although the pitch was very low, because of the large area covered, the roof created a field of color quite comparable to the field of color in the masonry walls. The commercial character of built-up roofing defeated the church design the architect had developed.

While we are considering materials for church building, it is appropriate that we consider not alone the materials seen from the exterior, but also those which create the reality of the interior of our church. It is here that the greatest skill and discernment on the part of the architect is necessary. It is here that by such skill the high ideals he hopes to present will be consummated. It is here that the committees, working with the architect, must cooperate to the fullest degree in order that the architect may accomplish desirable and fitting results.

Detailed discussion concerning materials used within the church will be reserved for the section dealing with the interior and its meaning.

The history of church building has been one in which rich and splendid color—in mosaic, in fresco, in stained glass, or in religious painting and noble furnishing—has abounded. The architect of today has those true and tried materials represented by masonry walls of stone or brick and the rich effect of beautiful woodwork, particularly in the treatment of roof-trusses and ceiling. He also has excellent modern materials, attractive in appearance and providing color. If used in dignified manner these materials are certainly suitable for modern church interiors. The architect has a wider opportunity than ever before to reach by means of well-chosen materials the fine quality of design necessary to the church. New heights, greater than those of the past, will be possible when we have developed the high artistry and emotional beauty which brilliance of design may contribute to the church.

The modern architect has in general chosen a simpler and more economical approach. Possibly he has chosen to go too far in this direction. Certainly, a richer use of color is desirable in place of the dull and timid use that prevailed in the generations immediately past. Clergymen and laymen should be open-minded in their acceptance of the architect's endeavor in this direction. They should acquaint themselves, by visits and examination with the many modern developments which have produced splendid work in fields other than church building during the past few years. From such examples a more churchly arrangement may be designed.

In smaller chapels, recently built, the walls and ceilings throughout nave and chancel have been of wood. Some of these have an intriguingly quiet charm. In other cases they show confusion and crudeness which repel rather than welcome.

There is no reason for us to hold that the interiors of our churches will no longer be built of walls and piers of cut stone or cut stone with brickwork, or brickwork alone. Masonry will continue to be suitable and satisfying, but for the interior of the church a great deal more care is required in choice of stone, and its designing, pattern, jointing and form, than is necessary for the exterior. The same is also true in the use of brick. Here a very pale, pink-grey tone can be handsome. Yet again, care in design, in coursing and in pattern is of extreme importance. We do not want an interior which is dull, nor do we want an interior commonplace in material and workmanship.

We will still continue to have interiors with plain plastered walls. These are the most difficult to use as means to gain the fineness we seek. Color must be given to overcome their plainness.

Even in the masonry-walled church we can look forward to wall treatments or facings which will bring about a greater interest, a greater beauty and a greater usefulness. Modern plywoods, modern plastics and modern textiles seem to invite the architect to search for a rich, harmonious beauty beyond that possible in plastered walls, and possibly more satisfying than masonry interiors of brick or stone.

Whether it be for the interior or the exterior, an excellent principle for the selection of material for our church is to choose material used in the locality in which the church is built; the better materials, the well-chosen materials, that are characteristic of that locality. This approach places the church as part of the community rather than separate from it. The finest skills, the most beautiful workmanship, the most handsome finishes of these normal local materials should appear in the church. By such an approach the church again becomes a leader in the education and elevation of community effort and taste. This is a function that is but a complement to the great religious truths the church sustains.

The knowledge of our materials will determine the quality of our design. Rich and beautiful building is the outcome of a thorough understanding of the qualities and the limitations of the building materials used in its construction. These indicate by their structural qualities as well as their beauty the manner of building. Of all building forms and building practices, the church is entitled to demand the fullest and soundest structural knowledge of its builders. The church is not a place for either makeshifts or untested experiments. It is appropriate to its importance that the church bear the stamp of intelligence of professional character. This is as real a challenge to the modern architect who would choose traditional form as it is to the modern architect who would choose new and different form. In either case it is his duty to know his materials and to use them with skill and with security. The church must be guarded from the expense of frequent replacements and unnecessary repair. It has a right to require of the architect that he express frankly the values and quality of materials chosen by him, citing both his own experience and that of other skillful men.

# BUILDING FOR USE AS WELL AS BEAUTY

As we near the completion of the preliminary plans for our church, we should check thoroughly to make sure that all portions of the building reflect truly the principle that we are building for use as well as for beauty. These two elements should be kept side by side, and throughout the building the finished work should reflect this understanding.

Reviewing our plan, we note that our first large mass had to be determined as to its shape and dimension by the number of seatings required for this church. This problem had to be solved correctly, and with it the space required within the choir and sanctuary. Here the practices of the church have a prevailing or predetermined pattern. The extent of the choir will depend on the number of choristers participating in the larger services. The extent of the sanctuary will be controlled by the area needed about the altar and the communion rail; or by the dimensions and position of a baptistry which is subject to beautiful solution when the ritual of the church accents that ceremony to a high degree.

Convenient to the choir and sanctuary areas will be the rooms for choir vesting and the sacristies for the minister and the altar guilds or other similiar groups. Each of these should be carefully studied to assure convenience, adequacy, and quiet.

Often the chapel is located near the sacristies in order to avoid duplication of facilities. The architect may find that the composition is enhanced by bringing the chapel to a more forward position, where, in the opinion of the clergyman and committee, it will better serve the purposes for which it will be used, even though a small amount of duplication is required.

An adequate entrance or narthex area is always needed. Too often this has been scarcely more than a tiny vestibule which has failed to serve many of the important needs of the congregation. Space large enough for a reasonable number of church members to linger after service is very desirable. Small and inconspicuous rooms opening off the narthex should be provided for brides' rooms and other conveniences needed at weddings and even at the normal services. The narthex should be wide enough to reach the doorways of the outer aisles as well as the doorway leading to the central aisle. Such width is not possible in all designs, but it is always possible to arrange a series of doors to give access to the narthex from the church by three openings rather than one.

In too many churches following traditional forms, a considerable number of steps must be climbed in order to pass from the outside walks into the vestibule or narthex. The traditional architect could not resist what seemed to him the attractive formality of the flight of handsome steps. These are a great inconvenience, and we should try to get along with the minimum number. Splendid plans have been prepared which have no more than three steps, or an 18-in. difference in level from the outside walks to the floor level of the narthex. At the top of these steps, whether they are as few as three or of a greater number, there should be a generous platform in front of the doors leading into the vestibule. The doors of the church must swing outward, and the members coming to service must have adequate space to enter without congestion. The width of the platform will vary with the size of the doors. Usually a minimum of 6 ft. is required to serve this purpose well. Within any church membership there is a considerable number of very regular and intensely loyal members who have reached some degree of infirmity due to age and failing eyesight. For these members the convenience of a vestibule level near to the ground is very real, and such planning is deeply appreciated by them. Similar convenience should be provided at the entrance to the chapel.

The connection of the church to the church school is most useful when it is direct. The clergy find it both practical and useful to plan their offices adjacent to the sacristies of the chancel on one side, and to the rooms of the church school on the other. This arrangement places them at a center convenient to both parts throughout the entire week. It works well if this portion of the plan can be reached directly, expresses a major entrance, and is inviting to persons coming to the church at times other than those of regular service.

The problem of providing for large attendance at the Christmas and the Easter seasons often leads to unfortunate adaptations within the plans. Because attendance at such services may be double or triple normal attendance, an effort is frequently made to tie in other sections of the plan for use at such services. As a general rule, a much more practical solution has been found in duplication of services on these festival days.

Providing space adjacent to the nave of the church, other than the chapel, is a possible solution to meet these unusual demands—but one practically never accomplished without a loss in the dignity and richness of the important services characteristic of these festival seasons.

Such adaptation is in no sense new. For more than a generation, churches have been planned in which either to the right or the left or at the rear of the nave, areas serving as classrooms or meeting rooms could be opened on the nave by means of folding doors or sliding partitions. These solutions have been discarded by the modern architect, primarily because they took away from the possible beauty and the emotional meaning of the church. They were impractical in use, leading to confusion rather than to convenience.

More and more the clergy and the building committees are taking the position that the sensible solution for numbers within the church should be determined by the fifty normal weeks of the church year, and that all planning should be to provide comfort, dignity and beauty within a nave which seats properly the normal, regular attendance. For those additional members who attend but two festival seasons, provision of loud speakers within the fellowship hall or other spaces should serve. Duplication of services within the nave is normal at such seasons and provides for these increased numbers.

The post-war developments of planning for this problem of greater area at times of unusual service requirements have been particularly interesting in connection with the new Jewish temples. In a number of recent instances large churches have planned extra spaces of almost identical dimension and proportion to those of the temple itself. By various devices of temporary closure, the temple has been separated from the adjacent social or fellowship hall, the purpose being that the areas shall open into one auditorium on the Holy Days.

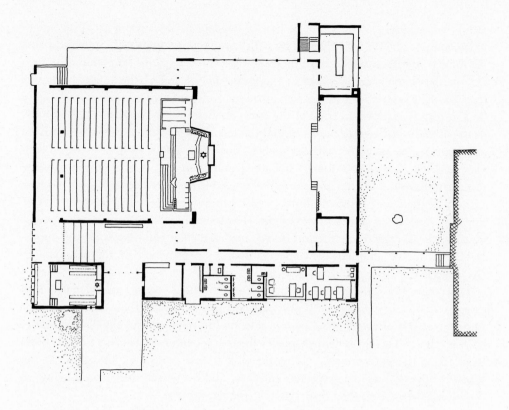

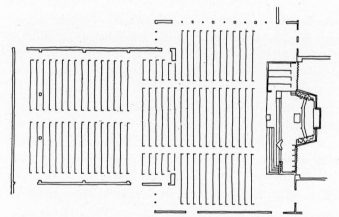

West End Synagogue, Nashville, Tennessee.
Percival Goodman, Architect. (Top and Center)

Temple Beth-El, Providence, Rhode Island.
Percival Goodman, Architect. (Below)

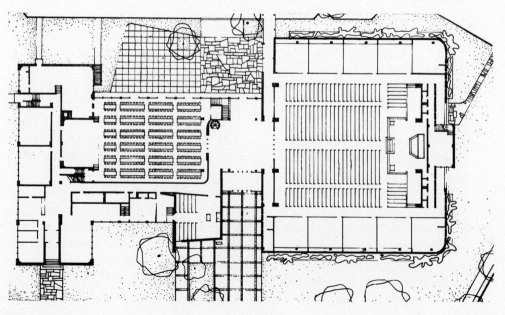

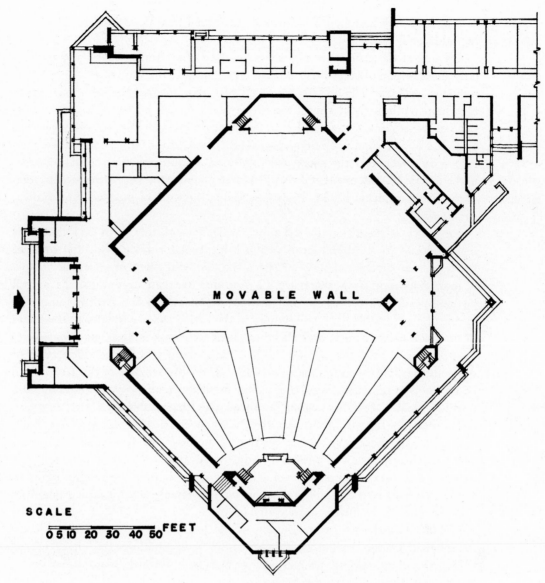

MOVABLE WALL

SCALE

0 5 10 20 30 40 50 FEET

*Emanu-El Temple, Houston, Texas. Gabert, MacKie*
*and Kamrath, Architects*

Two such solutions are indicated in the illustrations (page 44). One is that of the Temple Beth-El, Providence, R. I. The other is that of the West End Synagogue, Nashville, Tenn. Both of these buildings were designed by Percival Goodman, Architect.

Still another very recent solution continuing this type of planning has come to completion in the Emanu-El Temple at Houston, Texas, (above), by the architects Gabert, MacKie, and Kamrath. Their solution is rather novel in that it creates a large hexagonal room which can be separated at the center by means of a movable wall. Platform and Ark are placed at one end of the smaller sides of the hexagonal form, and the auditorium widens until it reaches the position of the movable wall. This space normally constitutes the temple. When the wall has been opened, the adjacent social center repeats in reverse the plan form of the temple. By this arrangement, provision is made to accommodate the greater number attending the temple through the period of the Holy Days of the Jewish calendar.

The other plan forms referred to in this connection are of a rectangular nature. The spaces open into each other by means of a system of folding doors or movable partitions. The various possibilities of such combined spaces lead to rather unique adjustments. In the Nashville temple, the platform and the Ark are built so that they may be rolled back from their normal temple position to the end of the additional space.

Any one of these solutions poses the question of appropriateness, and particularly the question of greater rather than less dignity at the time of most important religious services. The architect is faced with the fact that the additional space is to be used throughout almost the entire year for such purposes as social meeting, congregational dinners, and entertainment programs. For years this seasonal need has been solved with dignity—though possibly not with complete convenience—by means of large social halls grouped around patios or courts adjacent to the temple but not opening directly upon it. Such is the very attractive solution of the Temple Emanu-El, San Francisco, Calif., the work of Bakewell and Brown, Architects.

The more conventional of the religious leaders of this faith feel that it is inappropriate to combine areas planned for social service with the area of the temple at the very time when, from the doctrinal point of view, the temple is most important as a sanctuary. I feel that we can accept this as a well justified position. It seems to indicate that a plan which doubles the temple by means of a collapsible wall, will require in the added space a dignity of treatment in material, color, height, and all other elements comparable if not identical to the treatment within the temple itself. Thus, there will be no diminution of religious meaning when the entire area is used for the services of the Holy Days. In an entirely practical sense, this would indicate greater cost in building, and possibly greater formality within the social area than necessary.

The temple recently built for the Chicago Sinai Congregation combines modern design with appropriate dignity of architectural form (page 47). In this plan the confusion of temporary adjustment at the season of high religious meaning has been completely avoided. The areas within the temple are very large. The adjacent assembly room can serve in emergency for added numbers, and the very large foyer adds available space.

The fact that the post war solutions of the Jewish congregations have clearly accepted a greater space requirement within their buildings and have moved with increasing richness in permanent buildings toward adequate solution, justifies our optimism for the future.

An age is again approaching where true idealism in religion accepts the challenge to attain beautiful and complete architectural form. I wonder if this does not suggest an admission that our churches have been planned too closely to their minimum service needs; that they have failed to reach confidently toward a greater future. The simple but convincing provision of far more adequate space within the temple itself becomes no longer an impossibility. Such a splendid plan as that of the Chicago temple may indicate still further space enlargement by means of a skillfully designed basilican form, in which the dignity of wide aisle spaces surrounds the congregation at all its normal services, but adapts itself appropriately for added seating of the numbers attending the Holy Day services.

The mere mention of the problem of attendance greater than the normal requirement of the church, justifiably raises the question as to how the architect can provide in his plans for enlarging the seating provisions of the church at some future time without disfiguring that which has already been built. Scarcely any members of the clergy or of the building committee are willing to consider, in the medieval tradition, the possibility that a church might be built as part of a much greater church, and terminated at some point along the length of the nave so that it might be extended by another generation. Often if a large increase of seating requirements is foreseen at the time the first building construction is planned, the most sensible procedure is to leave off the entrance end (or west front), but modern churchmen do not like to build an unfinished church.

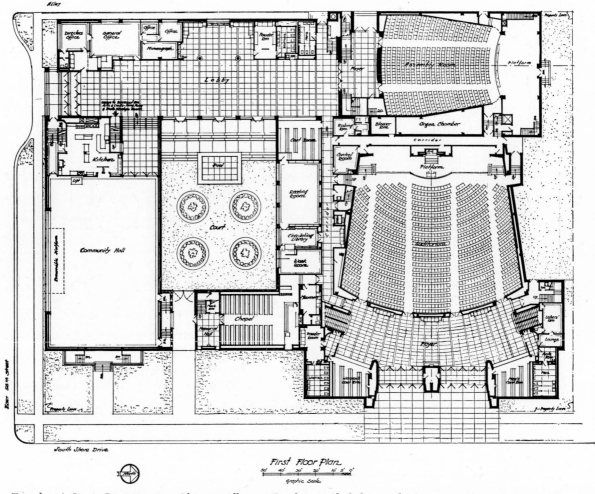

*Temple of Sinai Congregation, Chicago, Illinois. Friedman, Alschuler, and Sincere, Architects. Grunsfeld, Yerks, Lichtman and Koenig, Consulting Architects*

Lateral expansion is seldom satisfactory. I can recall many of the parish churches of England in which successive periods, possibly as much as a century apart, placed another aisle to the right or to the left until, in some instances, a five-aisle parish church was the result. These were interesting, historically, but not practical. Provision can best be made for further increase by placing the maximum accommodation required entirely within the nave. At some later time the church can be widened by removal of the side wall on one or both sides in the area nearest to the chancel. Suitable girders should be provided and built within the original walls, and the basilican piers in these particular sections can then be removed later without structural failure. The result will be a widened church with the additional seating at the most practical point. Such studies providing for future expansion should be recorded in the drawings with relation to those adjacent areas of the church school plant. In this way such expansion will cause the least expense and confusion.

As for the church school, its extent in plan will be of greater variety and less uniformity than is likely to be true of the church itself. Here our basic requirements are well-arranged classrooms which are well lighted and planned for convenience. The circulation should be free from confusion. The grouping of the various units will need a clear understanding of the manner in which they are to be used and the practices of the congregation at the time they are in use. The greater the flexibility we can provide in such planning, the more useful will be the church plant.

If the church school is to be only one story in height, its grouping around one

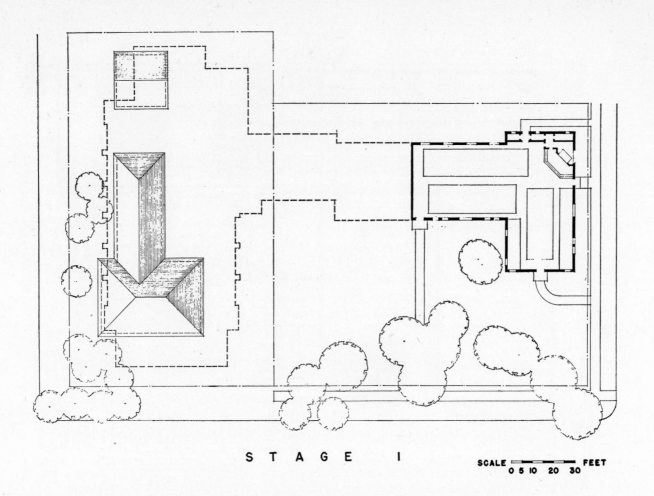

S T A G E   I

SCALE ⊢━━━┥ FEET
0 5 10  20  30

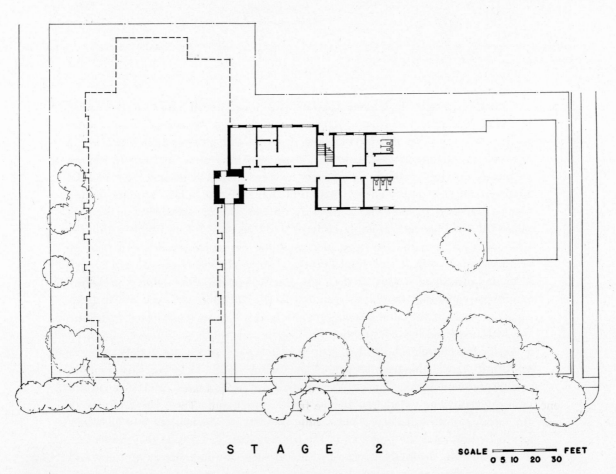

S T A G E   2

SCALE ⊢━━━┥ FEET
0 5 10  20  30

*Diagrammatic Development of Plan at Four Stages. Central Church of Christ, Houston, Texas.*
*William Ward Watkin, Architect*

48

or two courts or gardens is convenient and more attractive than a long strung-out plan. If, however, it is two stories in height, the extent at ground level will be less and smaller courts, or no courts, may be the most attractive solution, according to the nature of the site. The problems of noise and convenience are more difficult to solve in the two-story than in the one-story building.

It is important to repeat that we are trying to keep side by side the thoughts of usefulness and beauty in each individual portion of our plan.

We are trying to accomplish solutions not necessarily unique, unless the situations that call for them are unique. We are not deliberately trying to discard anything because it has been done before, if it was done well, but neither are we accepting because it was done before anything which by study we can prove could have been done better. All congregations want their churches to be beautiful, and they are perfectly right. Beauty which we shall attain if we are successful, will not necessarily demand financial burden beyond the means of the congregation, but will prove to be a perfect solution within the means and opportunities at our disposal. When church architects take this position, maintain it throughout, and have real architectural ability, the church which they design will reach true beauty.

Let me recall a recent example of the stages in preparing the plans for a church which was to be located on a moderately adequate site. The congregation had occupied a very small church with no additional plant available. Its physical properties did not justify remodeling and rebuilding The selection of the site was made with a view to a desirable permanent location in a well-defined residential area. The site contained approximately 40,000 sq. ft. and had a number of very beautiful trees. It also contained a two-story residence of considerable area located at one end of the property. The preliminary plans (page 48) were developed as shown. The intention was to use temporarily, with but slight remodeling, the rooms of the residence as rooms for the church school and offices for the clergy.

To advance the financial position for immediate building, commitment was made for the sale of the old church with delivery to be given as soon as the congregation could be cared for in part of the new, permanent construction.

The plans were laid out to provide for the necessary number of classrooms, offices, assembly rooms, banquet room and kitchen, kindergarten and nursery, and for a church building which would accommodate, when built, approximately 1000 seatings. The ideal solution seemed to be to retain as much garden area as possible within the site and to save as many of the handsome trees as possible, without deforming the plan. The plans (pages 48, 50) show the successive steps. They were really four in number, and could not be continuous in time due to the interruption of World War II.

The section at the right was built first. It eventually would be part of a two-story church school, but was so designed and framed that the second floor could be omitted and the area used as a temporary church auditorium. This would be adequate for approximately 400 people, and shows a neat but inexpensive arrangement of temporary baptistry in the sanctuary area (page 48). This section actually would consist of the permanent dining room, kitchen and pantry, permanent classrooms, kindergarten and nursery with several assembly rooms, and classrooms on the second floor. When stage one had reached completion, the sale of the old church was completed, and the congregation used the new church auditorium with its temporary arrangement.

The second stage in progress completed approximately one-half of the total classroom building. The other half could not be completed until the temporary auditorium was abandoned. It was necessary to build this classroom section as the second unit in order that the old residence on the church site could be

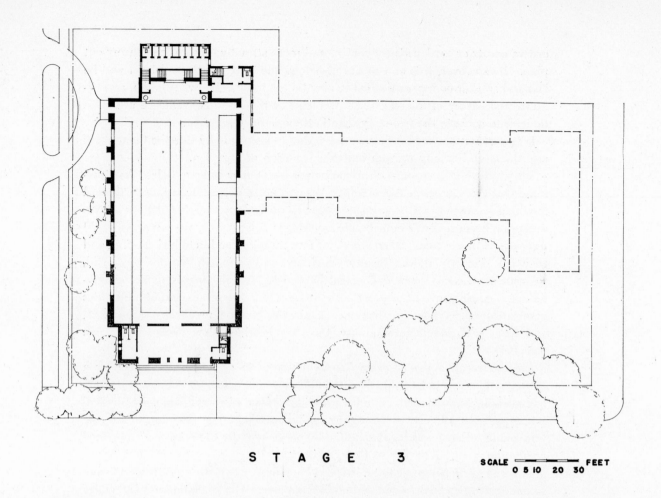

S T A G E   3

SCALE [scale bar] FEET
0 5 10 20 30

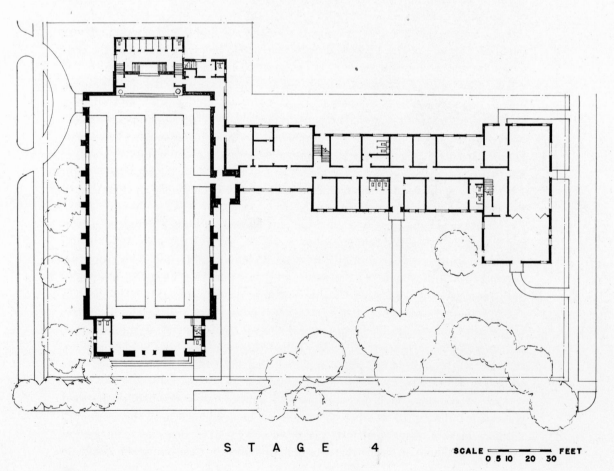

S T A G E   4

SCALE [scale bar] FEET
0 5 10 20 30

torn down and the building of the auditorium of the church begun. This plan was followed in all details and brought to completion before contracts for the church auditorium were awarded.

The third stage (page 50), came when the residence had been removed and the permanent auditorium was built. The work was carried to completion in all respects including furnishings, mechanical equipment and air conditioning, so that the fourth step in the progress of this church plant could be accomplished.

The fourth stage (page 50) consisted of taking out the temporary fittings in the portion of the church school which had been the first part of the whole plant, and building within it the floors, partitions, and finishes for the rooms originally planned for that section of the church school.

Except for the delay caused by the war, these steps could have continued in succession within relatively modest building time. Such solutions are often the most practical method of attaining the full plan. Sometimes the interruption between stages depends entirely on the financial ability of the congregation to meet the total cost. In this case it proved to be a very desirable solution in timing. The repeated building stages permitted funds to be available for each operation, and the time was to the financial advantage of the congregation. Their interest in eventually completing the entire group was sustained from beginning to end. This arrangement is one that an architect can undertake without fear of disappointment where it is impossible or impractical for the work to be undertaken in a single contract and the entire building to be built at one time.

Economy of cost was made possible by using an attractive but relatively inexpensive local brick, similar to that frequently used in good residential work in the vicinity, and because the design was confined to simple brickwork throughout, no separations or undesirable evidences of additions were apparent when the building was completed (page 53).

The most important value which the architect could give to work proceeding in stages as mentioned above was the decision to work very carefully for a complete plan, detailed in each of the different portions of the plant. Details were developed carefully with the building committee and the clergy, and accepted with enthusiasm by the congregation. The plans were drawn for the entire building as working drawings, and the specifications were complete, although supplemental and descriptive data describing the limits of work at each stage were necessary. It was very important not to build one piece at a time because that one piece alone had been designed. Instead, the entire building simply came into being in a slightly more prolonged manner than would be normal. The final result was as complete and direct as though it had all been in one contract. The changes or modifications were very slight and possibly even fewer than might have been required in one very large original building program. The time afforded allowed a financial freedom which permitted even more generous funds than first contemplated.

One of the very satisfying qualities in the group was the large amount of open lawn between the active city boulevard and the church school. The placing of this large building, two stories in height yet relatively low, was deliberate. It was placed away from the street for quiet, and in order that the great beauty of the old trees of the site might be retained. The committee's acceptance of this suggestion as it was developed in the earliest of preliminary drawings, gained rapidly and brought great enthusiasm. Their natural manner of thinking conceived of a building much closer to the lines of the property than the architect showed in his drawings. The results when built suggested landscaping which represented the equivalent of a generation's time. The sense of bare newness, so often felt in a church reaching completion, was absent.

Within the nave of the church that we have been describing, where seating is provided for 1100, great convenience was made possible by a slight incline in the floor. As the length of our nave from the face of the chancel steps to the rear wall at the narthex exceeds 100 ft., there is a sense of flatness which, while historically accepted, is an inconvenience within the modern church. When we can properly arrange our pews and stay within a limit of some 24 to 27 rows, we do not feel the need of change away from the flat floor level. As the distance becomes much greater, it is practical to give a slightly greater height to the nave floor at the rear than at the front. By this I mean that the rear row of pews is at a higher level than the front row of pews. In this example, where the total length involved was approximately 110 ft., a change of level amounting to 14 in., was used to great advantage. This was scarcely enough to cause the feeling of an inclined surface, but it was sufficient to give a somewhat greater visibility throughout the entire area than would have been true had it been omitted. The rise began with the fourth pew from the front of the church and continued back to the narthex, a continuous even slope. It caused no inconvenience in the placing of the pews.

Many years ago it was the opinion of Cram that the floor of the nave might possibly be given an incline rising toward the chancel; that if there were to be any change of level within the nave, the further elevation of the sanctuary and altar would add to its dignity. We know that if there is any inconvenience caused by an inclined floor it will be the same whether the floor rises or falls toward the chancel, provided the amount of incline is identical. The convenience for the congregation, especially those members seated near the rear of the nave, is greatly favored by the method suggested. If one seeks additional height at the chancel and again at the altar beyond the usual heights, this can be attained by additional steps.

The suggestion of slight incline to the floor of the nave is made in order to stimulate church builders to invite modern artistry, to give greater consideration to usefulness and convenience in their places, and at the same time to retain traditional religious emotion.

In modern practice, any auditorium or meeting hall is studied with regard to its proportions, its materials, and the manner in which the materials are disposed to achieve correct acoustics. In commerical work and in all other fields, not alone the larger rooms where many people assemble but also the smaller rooms are thought of and patterned so that the acoustics within the room will be satisfactory.

It is, therefore, very true that this element of church building deserves the foremost attention of the modern architect. The methods of design, the materials for use and the scientific service needed to accomplish desirable results—all of these are more universally available today than ever before. There is no reason why the architect and the church committee should not seek counsel of acoustical experts and follow their advice in connection with the church building. This service is important in small churches, but it is obligatory in churches of average and more than average seating requirement.

The materials available in the form of acoustical plasters and the many forms of acoustical tiles will develop interiors at least freed from reverberation. In order to use them properly, scientific counsel is required beyond the manufacturer's declaration of their qualities. In the field of the acoustical tile especially, much advance has been recorded in the last few years, and before specifying his material the architect should inform himself of the most recent improvements. Modern practice indicates two alternatives relative to design in terms of acoustics. One is the building of a live room, and the other is simply protecting it against confusion of sound. Wherever the live room has been carefully designed, it has proved very desirable.

*Central Church of Christ, Houston, Texas. William Ward Watkin, Architect. Photo by Shoemake-Stiles*

An amazingly successful solution in this type of auditorium was accomplished by the firm of Voorhees, Walker, Foley and Smith at New York in their Science Meeting Room, built in connection with the Research Laboratories of the Bell Telephone Company at Summit, New Jersey. The room was quite large, seating approximately 400 people. The basic development in the field of acoustics in this live hall was that voice volume as directed by the speaker on the rostrum did not have to be increased above that of speaking voice normally used within a relatively small room. It did not need any amplification by any mechanical means. On the other hand, the same voice volume directed from a point at the rear of the hall was reduced to but a small percentage of the volume from the rostrum. The rear wall was what we might unscientifically call a dead wall. All other walls were live walls, but patterned in such a manner that direct reflection of sound was avoided. The surfaces were of plywood running vertically and placed alternately at a modest angle instead of forming a flat surface. Whether the manner of the design chosen by the individual architect for the interior of his church be the live form or the more customary type, this example clearly proves the importance of designing the wall nearest the narthex to avoid a sound reflecting surface. We should study carefully the materials and form of the rear wall of our church.

Our objection to flat, or nearly flat, ceilings within the church is also related to acoustical design. The practice of placing an acoustical ceiling of industrial or commerical type above the nave may not be termed a solution of the problem. Such a ceiling defeats beauty within the interior, unless we go considerably farther and design an appropriate interest in shape and depth.

Scientific solutions of the acoustical problems have resulted in very unhappy forms in modern work. Such forms usually have the depth which is desirable from a scientific point of view. This depth is in no sense unfitting to the church, but the patterns suggested are often very unseemly for the quiet and the rich charm which is demanded in the church's interior. We may confidently declare that problems of acoustics will not be neglected by the modern architect, and we may as confidently hope that in cooperation he may advance with idealism beautiful designs which will serve in all respects the formulas of the experienced acoustical engineer. Modern work must be cooperative at the highest levels of knowledge.

Modern mechanical instruments for augmenting the power of the speaker's voice are very desirable. The modern church serves more completely if installations of this character are provided at the time of its building. A simple system of relatively small cost serves to make more comfortable and to relieve from embarrassment, not alone the clergy, but other speakers who visit the church during the year. The controls are so simple, requiring so little maintenance or repair that their use should be encouraged in all churches seating 300 or more within the nave.

With a microphone at the altar and one at both the lectern and the pulpit, the normal needs of the system will be well served. The control is most convenient when placed near the door from the narthex into the nave. At this position the head usher or one of his group is able to modify the volume to suit the quality of the speaker's voice and to reach the members seated in the rear of the nave.

The mechanical speakers themselves give the most pleasant effect if they are located near the chancel area. They take a small amount of room, and can be placed at a height approximately two-thirds the distance from the floor to the ceiling of the church. With care the architect can design attractive panels covered with beautiful grilles to avoid drawing attention to the mechanical nature of the system. It has been my experience that speakers so located serve in an entirely satisfactory manner a nave area seating nearly 1200 people. If the treatment of the chancel wall near the lectern and pulpit is carefully planned, it is not apparent that the voice of the speaker has been augmented by a mechanical device.

In churches in which the nave is of very great length, the system of amplification requires a great deal of study. Complete success is still to be reached. It is most annoying, almost fantastic, to be seated toward the chancel end of the nave with full visible awareness of the service at the pulpit or the altar, and yet have the voice or music seem to reach you from far overhead, or from eerie distances behind you. This distracting phenomenon is often due to the position in which mechanical speakers have been placed. Increasingly satisfactory acoustical equipment, and a greater variety appropriate for church use, will be developed from year to year.

From this short survey of the plan and space requirements which the architect must develop completely as he brings his building plans to their final working drawing stage, we realize both the importance and the quantity of the work which the architect performs. If he is to accomplish all of this detail in a thoroughly competent, imaginative, and forward-looking manner, the cooperation with the committee and by the committee must be very real during this stage of his work. It is here that all of the finer possibilities of his design are brought to reality. To reach such a result, the understanding of the component elements of use and beauty must remain dominant.

It is usually at the stage when the architect is reaching his working drawings that the need for decisions relative to cost, or decisions requiring economy, becomes very apparent. It is seldom possible to accomplish all that the architect would love to be able to accomplish. Therefore, decisions made at this stage often have a permanent undesirable effect upon the building. It is of extreme importance that those elements which cannot be changed or replaced at a later time without great expense, as well as annoyance, should be built permanently and beautifully. Those elements which represent degrees of finish or surface treatment (or easily-replaced temporary elements for which a finer permanent equipment is desired) are those which in emergency can be handled with extreme economy. It is necessary to hold first things definitely first, and to be determined, for the best interest of church community, that they shall not be sacrificed.

When an occasion such as has been described develops during the period of completing the working drawings, there is one further step that should be considered by the architect. I have found that it is very practical to analyze the drawings minutely for further simplification. It is amazing how often a series of relatively minor items of material or workmanship will be discovered whose usefulness is not demanding. A similar number of items will likely be discovered which can be modified without serious impairment either of use or of appearance.

The outcome of such a study is often revealing, even though it is not required for purposes of economy. It has the effect of stimulating the architect. It is, in effect, accomplishing a better design. Simplification is corrective. It brings about further refinement which is for the permanent good of the church. One would not expect the architect to find many opportunities for such decision, but it is my opinion that he enjoys them and their possibilities, especially if he is an enthusiast concerning the value of clean straightforward design simplified with the keenness of artistry.

# WITHIN THE CHURCH

It is within our church sanctuaries that architectural weakness has been most apparent. Almost universally throughout the past generation, architectural values of relative dignity have been reached in the church plant more often than within the church itself.

Failure often declares itself in the form, color, and material chosen to bring to reality the quality of our church. It is equally true that rich and warm emotional meaning is seldom expressed at this point of our work. The architect, as well as the layman and the clergyman will be judged by the degree to which a beautiful, devotional, and inspiring atmosphere is achieved in this, the major element of the church building.

For several generations the interiors of our churches have been commonplace almost to the point of dullness. Some have been so giddy that they are highly offensive to meditative and spiritual sensibilities. By and large, they have failed, and have often failed by a long way. It is said that this failure was due to lack of means, but I question this. Frequently the failure has been greatest where means seemed relatively abundant, if judged by the ornate form and ostentation scattered elsewhere throughout the plan.

Dullness has predominated, and it is our duty to see that dullness is discarded. Within our church we seek, by all the powers of architecture, to embody the rich faith of those for whom and by whom the church is built, and through the instrumentality of the church to render worthy service to our God. No lesser ambition justifies the building of a church. For its attainment, no effort of care, skill and thought can be neglected. Every ability we possess must be rigorously developed in order to achieve the most sensitive discernment of our problem.

The sacred shadowed space within the structure was, in truth the medieval church.

Every pier, every arch, and every vault was but the result of the increasing knowledge of the modeling of space fitting to express the essence of the church, its emotional meaning.

Within such space the happy, the thoughtful, and the sorrowful experience of man found joy or renewal of hope, as well as sweetness enriched by the long sequence of the church's continued comfort in generations past.*

Possibly the reason it has been so difficult for America to develop in its churches interiors which satisfy the emotional requirements of church building has been the lack of good examples scattered about the country.

* *Church of Tomorrow*, Harper and Bros., 1936, p. 135

We have had, here and there, handsome, beautiful interiors thoroughly fitting to the high religious purpose for which they were built, but these were infrequent and far apart. The churches that we use, the churches in which we were brought up, and even the churches which we have built have often lacked real conviction in emotional meaning, and have been pitiful expressions of the strength and significance of the Christian church

In our church building of today, we find the position of our architects quite different from that of the profession during the first three decades of this century. In those days the design of churches of importance seemed to fall within the offices of a relatively few men. In a way these men were making a specialty of church building. As the record shows, a number of them were very highly accomplished and their work reached dignity and permanent meaning, but by and large the church field was being formed by inexperienced men. Examples, other than a few photographs, were not at hand for their guidance. The more romantic Victorian work of masonry type constituted the large and important churches of their localities. Travel with the purpose of understanding church buildings, either at home or abroad, was infrequent. Those who did acquaint themselves with the possibilities of the church of their day by such study usually attached themselves to the offices of the prominent church architects. Gradually, this skill spread to wider areas of the country.

Today, coincident with church building in which we are engaged, we find large scale activity in all fields of construction. Larger works than those of the past are begun from day to day, or week to week in all commercial, educational, and housing fields. The offices are busy. What is more important is that the offices of young men are busy; busy with work of greater extent and promise than they could have anticipated at their present age had it not been for the accumulated building needs following World War II.

It is my opinion that we have reached the beginning of our era of church building with professional understanding appropriate to spiritual purpose. The reason I make this declaration is that the field is represented by many able young men, scattered uniformly throughout the country. In their work they had had probably only a few years' experience when World War II called them to the colors. With their return they brought the benefits of wider understanding, of wider travel, of more general meeting of people of diverse religious background, and, above all, a greater sense of personal responsibility and command. Because with the renewal of their practice there has been opportunity for church building, and because they have approached it seriously, there is being established a vast cumulative reservoir of skill in design of churches.

Not since the close of the Middle Ages has there been promise of such able advance in the building arts of the church. The universal longing of our people can be supported by a universal will to build and to give in order to carry out in new church buildings our cultural and spiritual ideals. Our people, universally, are determined that this shall be done. Steps which will bring the church's meaning to visible greatness are essential to our peace, our safety, and possibly our very existence.

It is especially in the planning and building of the interior that we must accept the commandment that completeness must be achieved. It is here that confusion must be avoided. It is here that the reality of service becomes part of the consciousness of man. No matter how simple or restrained our solution must be because of limited funds, the same high effort to design an interesting interior with spiritual atmosphere remains our objective. Time can be well and abundantly spent in testing and proving our design and its proportions. Later its colors, its finishes reached by the choice of this or that material, its correct

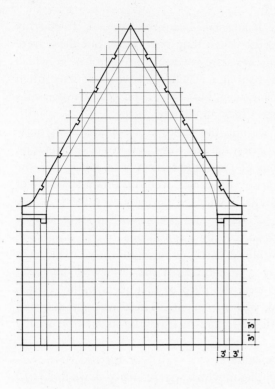

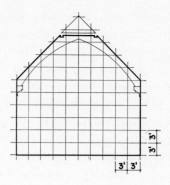

*Diagrammatic Sections:*
*Basilican Type (left),*
*and Chapel Type (above)*

lighting, will each require of the architect the same unstinting effort if the interior is to be a churchly one.

The central interest will reside in the chancel. Wrapped about this we shall compose, in order to enframe it, a church that does not compete against that major interest; that does not confuse by unnecessary variety, and does not offend by ill-shapen forms.

This does not mean that we seek rigid symmetry. It does not mean a likeness of form or color in the walls to the right and to the left as we face the chancel, for these can be undesirable. Close adherence to the pattern of traditional work, with symmetry, is found in many modern works, and not necessarily without reason. In other modern works, appropriate vistas which extend, rather than narrow, the fineness of the interior have been attempted. If rich meaningful interest can be secured by the lack of symmetry, it is to be recommended.

The basic principle which we shall keep constantly in mind in this, our modern

*Diagrammatic Section, Auditorium Type*

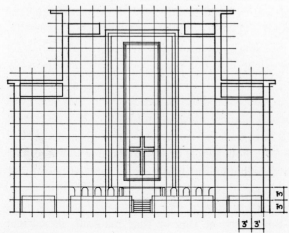

church, is that the architect should not allow its modernness to absorb his major attention. His attention should be restricted to holding above and beyond competition the architectural beauty of the chancel. The first requisite should be satisfying simplicity in design.

Too frequently, the external appearance of the church, (whether the building should appear like another church or look quite different) is more thoroughly considered and discussed by architect, committee, and clergy than the design and appearance of the interior, which is the church itself. I do not mean that the interior should or will preclude artistic external form in suitable material, color and proportion. Given the wide and able field of young church architects working seriously and understandingly to reach beauty within our church, the situation promises and prophesies far finer accomplishment.

Wherever possible, the clergy, the church committees and these young architects should visit with critical mind as many old and new churches as conveniently possible. They should visit these churches regardless of their ritual or likeness of service. They should seek to understand the completeness with which the building functions. Abundant notes should be taken as to those things which are desirable and those things which are not. In such a manner the alphabet of creative church building will be learned.

Since the war, professional practice has been accompanied by thorough research preparatory to drawing plans for buildings. This was particularly true in the study of postwar university libraries where a number of colleges, grouped together in common effort, gained advice and counsel in the solving of mutual problems studying the experience of the librarians on the one side and the architects on the other. Such research brought in many counselors from related fields. Efforts were made to evaluate possible innovations of great usefulness as well as beauty.

The attitude of mind which urges men to seek wisely and well the answers to their problems is a sane one. It could well be cultivated to a greater extent than in the past by the architects, building committees, and the clergy who are planning and building our modern churches, particularly in view of the relatively new problem of the use or adaptation of modern materials and modern invention.

Fortunately, this spirit of cooperation, placing value in the opinion of others, whose opinion is qualified or expert, is widely accepted. Many a backward or stagnant situation can be cleared to the point of understanding, possibly to the point of enthusiasm, if this open-minded approach is encouraged.

For the glory we seek within our church we wish our minds to be open, our hearts to be reverent, and our spirits full of inspiration.

A great human philosopher, the late Sir Henry Jones, Professor of Moral Philosophy at the University of Glasgow, very clearly reminded us:

We borrow the whole contents of our intelligence from the world in which we live, even our illusions, and we can create neither truth nor falsehood out of the emptiness of an isolated and self-closed mind. We must find room for the freedom of both mind and the world in knowledge; for both spiritual freedom and natural necessity in our practice; for both God and man in religion; for both individualism and socialism in our politics; for both the one and the many, the universal and the particular, everywhere.*

Our opinions of architecture suitable to our churches of today have found room for the freedom of both mind and the world in knowledge. It is fortunate, indeed, that this is true. A beautiful example of this in modern architecture is reported by Professor Murphy, who explains that when he showed his drawings and model of St. Ann's Church to Archbishop Ritter, they were endorsed by

* *Book of The Opening of the Rice Institute* p. 640

*Chapel, Parker Memorial Church, Houston, Texas. Herman Lloyd, Architect. Photo by Jack Richburg*

the Archbishop with the opinion, "This represents a new era. The Byzantine, Gothic and Renaissance served their time; it seems only right that a different architecture should serve our time."

With such open-minded approach we should compose the interior of our church in a manner reaching toward perfect proportion and beautiful simplicity. We may well start by considering the basic relations of its width and its height.

Too wide and too low a church will not develop our enthusiasm. We should have height at least equal to width. The effect of height gained by the lofty nave and the less lofty aisles has been a normal solution.

We often prefer to retain the form of the basilican church. We probably choose the more modern arrangement of smaller and lighter supports. Our effort is to control the width within the church as being within the pew areas. Such widths as are beyond the pews in the outer aisles we seek to treat as outside of this area and possibly of lesser height.

In my opinion we have failed to develop the advantage of the more lofty-ceilinged aisle. Why not carry the supports to a height nearly equal to the height of the nave, increasing the height of the aisle and using loftier window openings in the outer wall to achieve more unity as well as more interest?

Such proportions developed beautiful interiors in such vast cathedral buildings as those at Bourges and again at Palma in Majorca. Although the mention of cathedrals may seem inappropriate in connection with our more modest modern church dimension, their space design and concept are not limited to enormous spaces, but are equally appropriate to the more modest heights which we use today. There are many wonderful examples in the churches of the past of the composition of space within the nave, and of space within the aisle which create the lights and shadows, the interest, and the reverent qualities which are formed in these churches.

By means of the piers and aisles of the basilican type plan (page 58) the interest built up by loftier openings in the outer wall is refined. The lighting which comes into the nave by way of the aisle is softer. The church by its wider modeling develops the feeling of welcome which should be characteristic

**60**

*Chancel, Parker Memorial Church, Houston, Texas. Herman Lloyd, Architect. Photo by Jack Richburg*

of the church. The congregation is well placed, and the intimacy of the service in the sanctuary is very real; much more so than where only the outer walls determine the enclosing form of the interior.

In some modern designs this practice has been followed rather well on one side of the nave, but has been avoided on the other. This breaks the unity of the interior. The aisle is as desirable on one side of the church as on the other. With balanced aisles the circulation within the church is more dignified, more convenient, as well as more quiet; and the nave is given an identity which intensifies its meaning and unites it with the high interest of the chancel.

When planning smaller churches, the architect is likely to relinquish the charm of the basilican form. He will confine himself more closely to the chapel type, (page 58) in which the nave is enclosed only by the outer walls. In dealing with this simplest form, even higher artistry is demanded of the architect in order to produce a fitting and beautiful interior.

Walls must be more than bare, characterless enclosures. Depth, either physical depth or depth in color, becomes necessary, and it can be attained through the skillful choice and interesting use of material.

With this very simple chapel form, it becomes even more important that the nave and chancel become one in harmonious interest. Unfortunate effects have resulted from the use of high windows along one side of the nave wall with low windows opposite. Because these treatments are so near the pews, the difference is very noticeable to members of the congregation, and interest is taken from its proper position in the chancel. With serious study this difference of treatment in the two outer walls of the church may be resolved cleverly and well in a basilican type church where the aisle interrupts and modifies the abruptness.

**61**

Here the difference is not immediately apparent to the congregation, and the result is less self-conscious.

We may well expect that as the advanced modern solutions develop more beautiful interiors they will employ still more restricted window openings within these small churches. Possibly we shall reach the point where there are no windows at all. In secular work many attractive rooms serving different purposes have been designed windowless. Churches are already under construction in which the windows of the nave are being omitted. Problems of location, noise and traffic could justify this solution, but I doubt that these buildings will be as warm, rich and welcoming as churches which admit modest light through well-glazed windows, no matter how small the interior.

Two attractive, modern interiors are to be found in the new Parker Memorial Methodist Church at Houston, Tex. Here a complete unity of design has been developed in both the chapel and the church. In the chapel (page 50) the ply-wood finished walls are uniform from floor to ceiling, forming a rich and yet quietly intimate interior. Considerable height is expressed by this continuity of material. Had the treatment been broken into horizontal bands or changes of tone or color, it would have seemed much lower and less impressive. We find a similar uniformity in the treatment within the church proper, except that walls of brick have been used, with the chancel made richer in color by use of a plywood finish (page 61). The combination is very pleasing. In both cases the unity of interest is absolutely complete at the chancel end of the church. Examples of this character are becoming constantly more numerous in the work of the younger architects. The church referred to is the work of Herman Lloyd, Architect, Houston, Tex.

As compared with the desirable but warm simplicity we have been accenting, we occasionally find an austere conception of simplicity. By this I mean a rigid, hard, barren effect of masonry walls with accompanying severe, cruel furnishing. The idea may have been a misinterpretation of monastic simplicity, but the effect approaches a prison-like harshness. The ancient monasteries had simplicity, but they also had some of the greatest paintings, the greatest objects of religious art, within well-proportioned (though severely plain) chapels.

In the smaller churches there is a tremendous advantage in working stead-fastly for simplicity of form and color. Thus the architect unites the limited space so that it really appears greater rather than smaller. If the materials and colors bear refinement of taste, the result will be a much more impressive place of worship than would ordinarily be anticipated within strict space limitations.

A criticism by the clergy of modern church interiors has been that the low walls are dominated by exceptionally heavy ceilings. It takes time to reach the very best results. Modernism has tended to become imitative in all fields. Many of the churches built since the war have been very restricted in their means, and they may have sought too much. A more competent plan with a greater determination behind it, but requiring less initial construction, would have overcome this criticism so general among the clergy.

The position we have taken with regard to the interior being in truth the church is sustained by the position of the clergy. For them, the church is a changeless reality. The continuity of teaching the virtues of Christianity is not as of a day or of an age. Great wealth of meaning enwraps our civilization because of the continuity of the church. For that reason the greatest possible meditative value is necessary within the church for the inspiration of the individual.

It is very desirable, as well as very true, that the smaller church will always be with us. These churches whose dimensions seem to indicate chapel-like form are very close to the hearts of the people. For that reason their beauty

*Notre Dame Le Raincy. Auguste Perret, Architect. Photo by Andersen Todd*

can be a more intimate one. They will very truly carry the influence of their churchly quality into the mind and soul of our people and so enrich our civilization.

For these reasons I suggest great care be given to the design of the nave and chancel of the smaller church. As many of our younger architects meet this particular problem with creations approaching the simple, charming perfection that can one day be attained, a firmer foundation will be laid in the whole art of modern church building.

With larger churches we come to areas requiring the larger and wider nave. We no longer have the charming subtlety and intimate dimensions of the smaller chapels. Consequently, if the larger church is developed in the open but expanded chapel plan, problems are certain. In a very wide nave, natural lighting by means of large windows on both sides usually produces a feeling of void in the heart of the church.

The wide nave is difficult to compose and crystallize toward an emotional quality. Often natural lighting must be supplemented, even for daytime service, and it is therefore logical to diminish the window areas. The treatment of the wall surface must be deeper, quieter, and more continuous so that the apse space, which is intended to dominate the entire picture, will be accented without separation.

In the nave of our church we are seeking to reach by creative imagination an expression of our longing and devotion to Christian service and all that it means in lasting value. For this reason we dare not be either boastful or playful; we must accept the obligation to be serious. We are challenging ourselves to reach our very best, to refuse to be limited by timidity, weakness or dullness, and to advance with the spirit of high endeavor.

We shall accept the fact that the proper design of the nave is a serious and a difficult problem. We find a true basis on which to work in the demand for orderly simplicity. Let us take the interior of the Cathedral of Amiens, which is probably the finest of all church interiors. As compared with the multitude of

*Christ Evangelical Lutheran Church, Minneapolis, Minnesota. Saarinen, Saarinen, and Associates, Architects. Photo by George Ryan Studios*

medieval churches and with the many great cathedrals, Amiens appears, as we stand within its lofty nave, to be the most simple, the most easily built, the most clearly understood work of the greatest period of Christian building. When we analyze what causes it to seem so very simple, structurally restful, and artistically quiet and graceful, we shall find that there is harmony, to the degree of likeness, in proportions prevailing throughout the whole cathedral nave, trancepts and choir. The proportion of the width of the piers and their arches to their height in the aisles of the Cathedral is carried in like proportion throughout the nave. It is repeated, with modest change, in the proportions of window openings, whether they be the windows of the aisles or the clerestory windows far above. In other cathedrals, such as Notre Dame in Paris or the cathedral at Reims, these forms are not so insistently harmonious; the proportion and shape of the arches and the openings vary considerably. The whole range of evolution through the periods of the early Romanesque, through the Transitional period on into the Gothic, proved the designers groping step by step toward such architectural serenity as was finally reached in the forms of Amiens.

The parish churches as well as the larger city churches of the later Gothic period hold maximum interest and beauty when they, in turn, employ this consistent proportion. Where their forms are varied, although not necessarily clumsy, fine emotional values are wanting.

When later ages chose by revival efforts to recapture the splendid quality of medieval work, they could not understand this simple but supreme solution. Attractive windows chosen by eclectic preference from one example or another, were composed and combined with good piers and good arches chosen from another attractive example. They were not chosen for likeness of sensitive combination. Good in themselves, they often competed strangely with each other. Such distinct elements as piers and arches on one hand and windows and doors on the other were put together not because they really fitted together, but because the designer liked them as individual parts. The church as a whole seldom related correctly either to the proportions of its windows and doors or to the proportions of its piers and arches. The result could be said to be historic, but certainly not in the sense of recapturing a great architecture.

Applying this thought directly to designing the nave of our modern church, let us proportion carefully each form to the other forms within the building. We shall not want wide, flat rectangles in one part of the design and tall, slender rectangles in another part. We must find proportions that fit our particular dimensions and needs, and try to refine them to a point that is interesting and to relate them to elements of lesser dimension which can retain likeness of proportion. Starting in this manner, sketching, tracing and sketching again, in the usual way of studying a design, we can develop an expanding and inviting openness by which we can approach a beautiful solution.

In line with this suggested approach, our use of windows will become a controlling factor. We must decide very early to what degree large or even excessive glass areas will add to, or detract from, the picture we have set before us. Here we have two modern practices prevailing. One sheathes our nave and chancel with great fields of glass occupying more than half, possibly two-thirds, of the entire wall surface. An example of this use of glass appeared years ago in the Church of Notre Dame Le Raincy, by Auguste Perret (page 63). It represented an understanding of emotional design carried down from the days of the Sainte Chapelle. Unfortunately, the great skills necessary to produce glass pattern rich in color, simple in design, and fitting for the nave of the church are extremely rare today. Without going into detail as regards the practical elements of both acoustics and of cost, we may safely say that in order to reach true excellence, the extensive use of glass in the nave will require skills and means far greater than normal.

The other prevailing form (page 64) tends to limit window openings to a smaller area than was allowed in traditional architecture. In this form the window becomes a long, slender opening either repeated at wide intervals corresponding to bay distances within the church, or placed in groups at intervals corresponding to bay distances. With this form the unity of design, the unity of materials and the unity of color values throughout the church are all more easily attained than in the church which is dominated by glass.

The stained-glass window has been very deservedly decried by modern architects. The stained-glass window of great beauty and color tended, in the works of the past generation, to follow directly the patterns of the medieval glass of either England or of France. It satisfied the donor far more than it satisfied the members of the congregation. The fact that the donors played so large a part in making possible the stained-glass windows led to the diversity of windows representing, characteristically, the temperamental diversity of donors. Here and there consistent patterning was attained throughout the church, but this was far from the usual practice. It was inappropriate, at best, to fill the openings of a modest church with costly colorful glass of historic pattern when the entire picture within the church, except for the windows, was a simple one reaching hardly beyond an intimate homeliness.

Colorful light, properly used, in proportions to give a jewel-like interest which is secondary and not primary to our total composition of the interior, should be welcomed, and I believe that nearly every young architect working toward modern solutions is of this opinion. The difficulty is to choose our color scheme, its pattern, and to determine to what degree this can provide religious meaning appropriate to our day. We are convinced it should not imitate the patterns of windows of the past. In all the fields of religious art there has been a stagnancy.

*East Liberty Presbyterian Church, Pittsburgh, Pennsylvania. Cram & Ferguson, Architects. Photo by Haskell*

A certain degree of skill was reached more than a generation ago, by which the finer qualities of thirteenth century glass were attempted. When the patterns changed to glass and design representing the religious thought of our own age, they seemed to fail sadly. With the wide range of church building we are now facing, architects, laymen, and clergymen must promote enthusiasm among craftsmen capable of giving us religious art, stained-glass, finer furnishings of our chancels, sculpture in wood and stone and religious paintings that are serious and stimulating.

The design of our ceiling, possibly the largest surface in the building, is of primary importance. As an unbroken surface, it will destroy the entire picture. The medieval church found its greatest beauty in its lofty vaults, among which was the constant play of light and shadow, all deeper in tone than the light at the level of the congregation. If the church was not vaulted, the intricacies and skills of exquisite carpentry were reflected in the workmanship of the wooden ceilings. Whether these were of steep open form which added greatly to the height of the church, or were modified so as not to remain open for the full height, they still were interesting and relatively deep in color. It is a fact that both the vaulted and the carpentry-roofed interior had deep rather than light tone for their ceilings.

If we think in terms of the colorful ceilings of the Renaissance, which were often made of plaster, we find that they were neither flat and formless nor pale in color. Usually they had a modest curvature. If they were flat, they were deeply coffered with many moldings and many panels large and small. They were brought to completion in tones that we might describe as an overall blue-grey of considerable depth. This was not a monotonous tone because it was a color made of many colors, of many designs and many painted panels as well as painted moldings. The richness of this painting did not conflict with the color richness of the sanctuary. It was a richness, however, that created a meditative quality within the church.

The modern solution of the ceiling is not likely to be the masonry vaulted interior. Certainly such solutions will be infrequent. Excellent solutions by means of the timber-trusses, either of the more traditional types or of the more open laminated truss forms, indicate that the wooden ceiling will continue in a great number of cases. Where it is entirely a treatment of wood for the facings of the ceiling as well as for the trusses and their members, the color value remains deep. Still more color enrichment, as we recollect the use of color on the wooden roofs within the churches of Sicily, could be welcomed. It has been true that in quite a number of the very modern designs, in which the wooden truss was used to gain height, the ceiling itself has been of plaster or other modern material simulating plaster, and has been finished with light tones so that there is no depth in the ceiling. The anatomy of the wooden members is declared in an offensive way. If the ceiling is to be of wooden trusses, we may well choose to hold to tones characteristic of wood, even though the ceiling areas may require acoustical treatment with other materials.

The most disastrous problem arises when we have a plaster ceiling which is practically flat. Unless we can put more design and study into this, we are wasting our efforts within the nave. First, we must break up its flatness. The manner by which we do it must be one appropriate to the forms which create the pattern of our interior. These may be forms that we choose to have run from narthex toward sanctuary as a series of planes, either of plaster or combinations of plaster with wood, by which we build up a design interest which is quiet but interesting. The more acceptable membering of the ceiling seems to be that of using panel and beam forms across the width of the church, running from one side to the other and keeping some rhythm suggested by the pattern of our walls. There will be an advantage in the depth and scoriation of the ceiling. Whatever the solution, it should permit the treatment by means of either the natural color of the material itself or by color applied, to give a ceiling which is relatively deep in tone. A light ceiling seems to rest upon our heads. A darker ceiling is less apparent and accents the brighter tones and greater light which should abound within the sanctuary. The ceilings within our churches and their possible merits or possible demerits are far more definitely explained or apparent if we visit the churches at the time of the evening service. With a bright ceiling, the interior sinks into pale nothingness, and much of our effort to create a beautiful sanctuary fades from the picture. We understand clearly how this failure to solve the ceiling is a defect obvious in the day services as well. It is the overall picture of solemn interest in one unified creation that we strive to know clearly and to make possible.

The dignity of the vaulted ceiling gives to the church a grandeur which is not attained by any other means. Vaulting shafts, vaulting ribs and vaults seem to have passed from the picture of the modern church. The passing may be but temporary. Solutions like those shown on page 66 challenge us to find in modern terms a fullness of interest equal to the splendid vaults of the past. Let us hope that the church will declare itself forever willing to be daring. No beauty which we can conceive is too great to be the fitting attribute of the church. "The true role and destiny of architecture is to express without mitigating its human and utilitarian ends, the highest thoughts of man, the quality of its civilization, and to satisfy with durable creations the feeling and desire for the eternal which each man possesses in himself." Such was the philosophy of Andre Lurçat.

It is within our church that architecture should reach its most full and complete expression and declare its power to bring into physical embodiment the longings of the spirit within us. It is possible for architecture to express nobly those longings with rich, eternal meaning which can be possessed again and again, generation after generation, by those whom the church shall shelter and who shall come to it seeking quiet, meditation, and inspiration.

# THE HEART OF THE CHURCH—THE CHANCEL

The chancel area includes the choir and the area beyond the choir in which the altar or the baptistry is placed. In this area beauty above all other beauty within the church should be sought and reached. The completeness with which a dignified and inspiring solution is attained in the chancel will represent the fulfillment of the church's meaning and aspiration.

Throughout all the history of church building, the major interest has been at this, the eastern end of the plan. The practices of the church, its devoutness of ceremony, and its major visual interests have developed in this portion of the church building. The heaviest masonry, the richest arrangement of piers and arches, and the finest vaulting of the ceilings have been centered in the area of the chancel. Whatever the ritual of the church may be, it is here that we have our opportunity to express it by fitness to use and beauty. Its materials, the skill of the workmanship, and the appropriateness and dignity of furnishings invite the maximum cooperation of the creative artistry of the architect and the idealism of the clergy. Traditionally, the chancel was the first portion of the church to be built, with the building progressing westward from the chancel until it reached completion at the west front. Although our modern methods of building seldom indicate so prolonged a system of masonry construction as to require the building of the chancel as a separate initial portion, may I suggest that if the traditional primacy and sequence of building were again clear to the designing architect, his interest in the chancel might hold greater meaning. He would avoid the confusion or underemphasis which arises when he designs the church first. In certain of the more modern churches, for example, we feel that the eye of the designer slipped to the right or to the left, giving undue emphasis and greater novelty to one or another of the sidewalls of the church, and relegating the chancel to secondary interest.

In the later Romanesque and the Gothic work of Europe, a depth was added to the architecture of the chancel by the ambulatory aisle, a passage for circulation around and behind the piers of the chancel. The chapel or chapels were served by means of that aisle. Seldom in the modern church do we have a need for more than one chapel, and we seldom place it in the historic location. It should be interesting to try plans which give the same usefulness to the chapel, as accomplished in other modern positions, but place it on an axis behind and beyond the chancel.

Later, in the traditions of England particularly, and to some degree in the northern countries, the end wall became rather dull because it was flat. This

*First Methodist Church, Midland, Michigan. Alden B. Dow, Architect. Photo by Bradford La Riviere*

was less satisfying than the chevet that the French had used in their Gothic work. There were, however, numerous examples that were pleasing if not convincing. The solutions in church building of recent generations have been varied, and for the most part confusing. In some instances the end of the church has been completed by placing a raised choir, visible to the congregation, behind the altar. Seldom has this solution been fitting or sightly, or has it carried sufficient dignity to express meaning in the church. Access to and from such choir space is informal. It develops a certain degree of confusion and noise, and the visible choir forms an inappropriate background for the preaching service. We should plan to overcome such distraction. We should substitute a splendid unity of design and refined enrichment, with symbolism which will express the ideals and the religious theories of this particular faith.

The design of the chancel gives embodiment to the ideals and aspirations of the church. Definition of intent is the obligation of the clergy; beautiful expression of this intent is the obligation of the architect. For the most part the weakness in American church building has been the lack of clear definition and corresponding clarity of expression in the chancels of our churches. Ornament, statuary and other decoration could do little to improve a meager, ill-formed chancel space, and under these conditions the maximum spiritual interest within the church could not be reached.

Amazing progress toward strengthening this weakness has been shown in our churches of the past decade. It is a splendid tribute to the skill of the modern architect that he has been able, in the majority of cases, to recover the primacy of interest and meaning in the chancel. In my opinion, this recovery promises a brilliant future in the field of modern church building. Possibly the first steps have been toward an unnecessary degree of severity, but the architects have clearly demonstrated their understanding that the altar or the baptistry represents the heart of the particular church which they are building. We no longer build ornate, meaningless architectural forms which enshroud the altar or the baptistry. We are willing to give these elements the full, clear declaration they deserve.

It is doubtful that the churchmen of today realize the extent of the recent advance toward this rightful emphasis, as compared with the confusion existing a generation ago, when the central pulpit often blocked out any possible emphasis of the altar.

The central pulpit was most beautifully adapted to the services of the Unitarian churches. In these churches the primacy of the pulpit was appropriate, representing the embodiment of moral and ethical attitudes of conscience. The sacramental meaning of the baptistry and of the altar did not appear in such chancels.

Generally, however, the acceptance of the altar as the center of worship and of the pulpit as the center of intellectual and spiritual guidance has become very real. Among nearly one hundred new Protestant churches there were but four planned for central pulpit location, and I learn that in one of these four the pulpit position was moved from the center before the church reached completion.

Unity in design means complete unity. Such unity has often been defeated by a horizontal band, such as wainscot of oak or other rich material, above which were simple walls finished in plaster or perforated for window openings. Unity is as real in considering height as it is in considering length. If we choose our material and study our design for a composition which is unified by vertical accent and not broken horizontally into two or more planes by different materials, we simplify our problem even if we do not solve it at once.

This design form, which constitutes the end of our church, is fundamentally the proper background for the principal element of the church's interest, its altar or its baptistry. We should design with the altar or baptistry known, and its form and dimension determined within reasonable limits of change. We will then be creating a single unified picture to which we hope to have the ability to give true, religious meaning.

Such a unified picture has been developed in the interesting design of the chancel for the First Methodist Church of Midland, Mich. (page 70). The chancel itself is very direct and simple in its form. It accents very clearly the altar as its principal interest. The pointed ceiling panel continues unbroken throughout the nave and ends in a sky window developing the maximum lighting at the chancel.

The entire space within the chancel, including both the choir area, if there is to be a choir, and the sanctuary or altar area, should be as free from changing forms as we can make it. The greater richness, it is true, may be held to the end wall, but we should not change rapidly to other materials. Rather we should tend to unify, by similar materials used in a plainer manner, the entire wall area within our chancel. All this only serves as the proper background for those pieces of useful furnishing and equipment which make possible a beautiful service within the church. Our goal should be to contribute to the greatest possible meaning of this service.

In many of the more modern designs, one feels that the interest in the east

*Church of the Epiphany, New York City. Wyeth & King and Eugene Mason, Associated Architects. Photo by Louis H. Dreyer*

wall has been truly studied, although the solutions by which this was accomplished differed greatly. Often when this wall has been successfully designed, change comes too quickly as one turns to the side walls of the chancel.

It is entirely appropriate that the overall richness given to the chancel should be different in material, in height, and refinement from the walls throughout the nave of the church. This may be a difference of material, a difference in color, and a sensitive difference in enrichment. After all, the chancel is a relatively small area. The number of square feet of costly material, required to solve it well, is not a large item in the total cost of our church plant. We should spend money intelligently, spend it where it is appropriate to spend it, and we should also be economical where it is appropriate to be economical. The chancel is not the place where it is appropriate to be economical.

Equally important with the other rules that we have set for ourselves is a

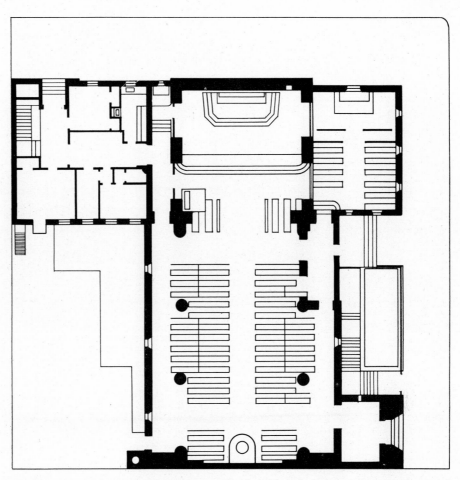

*Church of the Epiphany, New York City. Wyeth & King and Eugene Mason, Associated Architects*

thorough study of the manner in which the nave opens into the chancel; or, in reverse, the manner in which the chancel opens into the nave. Historically, when the arcuated forms prevailed in church building, this opening was determined by a large arch which, with its piers, was narrower and less high than the normal cross-section of the nave in front of it. This was characteristic of churches of moderate dimensions—parish churches rather than cathedrals. Continuous ceiling forms through nave and chancel may be satisfactory. If, however, there is to be a form creating a structural separation of the chancel area from the nave area, then this form should fit well with the design of the chancel space and not conflict with the general form of the nave.

Very interesting solutions have been developed in smaller churches which have added a new interest. One particularly successful example is the small Church of the Epiphany in New York City, the work of Wyeth, King and Eugene M. Mason, associated architects (pages 72, 73). The church is in a built-up area of the city and on a very limited site. The architects have chosen to give greater height to the chancel space than to the nave. They have marked the church with a tower which is the same dimension as the chancel. This tower, rising sufficiently above the roof of the nave to give very attractive lighting as well as dignity, is the eastern end of the church. The extra masonry necessary to raise the tower was needed to develop good exterior design. It was more appropriate than a tower form without usefulness would have been. Consequently, we see that use and beauty side by side guide us to good work.

The arrangement of the plan of the chancel space develops from the nature of the ceremony of the particular denomination for which we are building. The

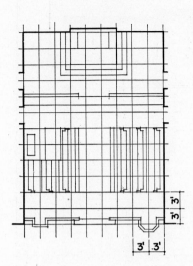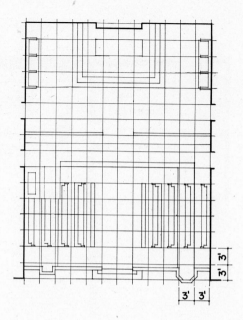

*Modular Plans of Chancel (far left); of Chancel Space (left)*

accent in the majority of cases is upon the altar. In the Protestant churches whose service requires a vested choir, the choir is usually grouped on either side of the wide central aisle leading from the chancel steps to the altar. The schematic diagram (above) indicates the more usual space requirements of the normal parish church in which the altar rather than the baptistry is the principal element. The diagram follows the 3-ft. grid pattern indicated in connection with areas within the nave or auditorium of the church.

In many churches the baptistry is the primary element of the chancel. As such it deserves dimensions fitting to its primacy. It should not be confused by any visual interference caused by other furnishings. A schematic diagram is shown on page 75.

A seemingly simpler but really more difficult condition arises when no choir is required within the chancel. In certain denominations this is the prevailing practice. The baptistry gains in interest under these conditions, provided the space within the chancel is not needlessly reduced, but continues to have rich depth which will give dignity (page 75).

Catholic churches have usually been generous in the sanctuary area. Even though the choir is not placed in this area, its width and depth bear more generous proportion to the areas within the nave than is true in Protestant churches. Most recent designs of Catholic churches have presented this primacy of the altar within the sanctuary area with increasing beauty and with richness but simplicity.

The dimensions of the chancel will be much smaller if we are planning a chapel rather than a church. The chapel does not usually have space for choristers, unless it is of dimensions and seating requirements approaching those of a small church. Because of the small dimensions characteristic of the chancel area in the chapel, we are called upon to seek a more intimate quality in the design of our altar and other furnishings. Such intimacy occurs in the interior of the Chapel of Christ Church Cathedral, Houston, Tex. (page 76). The Chapel has been given considerable height in proportion to its relatively small dimensions. This has proved very satisfying, and adds to the rather extreme simplicity of the architecture.

As we move from the smaller chapel form to the small church, the area within the chancel increases rapidly. An excellent example is the chancel of the Church

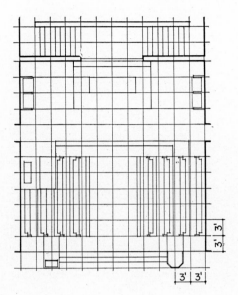
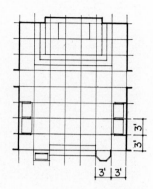

*Modular Plans of Chancel (right);*
*of Chancel Without Choir (far right)*

of the Epiphany, where great height, added dignity and extremely well-planned lighting of the chancel give it maximum interest.

As we pass to churches of average or greater than average seating requirements, the chancel areas should increase proportionately. This greater dimension, as well as greater richness of ornament, is characteristic of the stylistic treatment shown in the chancel of the West Liberty Presbyterian Church of Pittsburgh (page 77), designed by the firm of Cram and Ferguson. The excellent stone architecture has been carved with fitting ornament, and the stone reredos, decorated with the magnificent sculpture by John Angel, brings to realization the skill of the designers.

For the church of today like dignity can be reached, although the forms may be very different. From a photograph of the interior perspective of the First Baptist Church of Longview, Tex. (page 79), we see a chancel of very modern feeling which is of great simplicity in form and material. The walls, both interior and exterior, are of brick. Its architects are Wilson, Morris and Crain, of Houston.

The chancel can be unified in a very direct manner by its majestic lancet window. This window, properly glazed with glass of jewel-like quality rather than that of figure-window type, can be the dominant note of the entire interior of the church, and in this manner reach spiritual quality appropriate to the vast chancel.

In designing the chancel the architect must plan for a suitable and adequate space for the church organ. The manual will be placed in the choir area. The organ chamber normally has been at a second level, above the sacristies. The architect proverbially tends to allow too small a space, both in floor area and height, for an installation of the organ. Adequate clearances are necessary for the repair and upkeep which are very constant in connection with church organs. If the church be of more than very modest dimensions, an area less than 20 by 20 ft. should not be considered adequate. Height ranging from 18 to 20 ft. is usually required. The organ manufacturers are skilled in adapting their installations to inadequate spaces, but the quality of the organ is usually impaired when the architect has failed to give careful study to space requirements. It would be well, if the architect could do so, to plan more space than required by the

*Golding Chapel, Christ Church Cathedral, Houston, Texas. William Ward Watkin, Architect. Photo by N. E. Barrick*

initial organ installation. Additional sections, providing additional stops, are often acquired later for a more complete church organ. It is well to make provision for such expansion if the space can be arranged conveniently.

From the point of view of the design of the chancel, the major problem is the passage of sound from the organ to the chancel and nave. The very large openings needed for the organ present a perplexing picture. They can become annoying in appearance. The older types of organ screens, with pipes combined, have been abandoned. The proper solution seems to require simple openings of adequate total area, moderately divided in a design appropriate to the forms of finish in the chancel.

The position of the organ chamber, whether to the right or to the left of the chancel, will determine the position of the organ manual in the choir. Organists prefer nearly unanimously to be seated on the side of the choir facing the organ chamber, rather than directly below.

There are a great many examples in which the placing of the organ manual, while attractive to the architect in laying out his choir plan form, has been so

*Apse, West Liberty Presbyterian Church, Pittsburgh, Pennsylvania. Cram and Ferguson, Architects. Photo by Arthur C. Haskell*

serious a defect in use that considerable cost has been incurred in rebuilding a portion of the choir furniture to permit the placing of the manual in a satisfactory location. The organist has the problem of directing his choir. In the normal position of the manual, he sees directly in front of him the majority of the choristers. The other choristers have their backs toward him. This difficulty is solved by placing several small horizontal mirrors above the choristers opposite the organist.

It is well to plan a convenient method of entry and exit by the organist to his bench at the organ manual. The organist plays a far more important part in the scheme of things in church building than the architect might anticipate. Often his views are rather adamant. It is appropriate that the mechanical problems (if we care to call them that) of presenting church music be properly coordinated by a thorough study on the part of the architect, so that this very real element of the church service will not suffer from defective planning and installation.

In view of the space required for the organ chamber with space for possible later expansion of the organ, mention should here be made of the use of the church tower as an organ chamber location. This location was rather general a generation ago, but it was unsatisfactory except where the tower was large. A tower can seldom be in good proportion in mass and design when it contains space inside its walls as large as that required by an organ chamber. When the architect chooses to use a second level of a tower as an organ chamber, it should be so arranged that there is space adjacent to this second level which can be combined with the area within the tower so that the organ chamber may not be restricted below its practical needs. A tower of a church of modest requirements will seldom exceed 18 x 18 ft. in outside dimensions. Its slenderness ratio will demand unusual height when the dimensions of the square of the tower are increased. Possibly this height will be inappropriate. In fact much more pleasing forms seem possible where the exterior width dimension of the face of the tower is limited to some 14 to 16 ft.

Possibly the reason for the use of tower space in so many examples lies in the fact that it is extremely pleasant, in mass and grouping, to place the tower at the internal angle of the church school and the church. This tends to bring the tower nearer the position of the chancel. This plan can be and has been worked out well. At all events the architect should put down as an object of important study the fact that the church organ is part of the church, that the organ manual is part of the choir, and that these have bearing upon his design.

Concerning the levels in the chancel, these will vary according to the ritual of the church which is to be built. Probably the most accepted and normal sequence has been that of a change of level from the nave floor to the floor of the choir of three steps of 6 in. each or 18 in. At the end of the choir, with adequate passage between the ends of the choir stalls and the communion rail, there is normally one step representing the kneeling level at the communion rail. Within the sanctuary, it is usual to elevate the altar three steps of 6 in. each, or an additional eighteen inches. Therefore, the most normal change of level is 3 ft. 6 in. for the level of the floor at the altar above the level of the floor of the nave.

If the altar is not used in this central location, but the space is occupied by a baptistry, the three steps to the altar are omitted. Handsome arrangements are on record where, even though there be a baptistry of excellent design and primary religious and emotional interest, it has been placed at a sufficient height so that the altar may be placed immediately in front of it. Under this arrangement, a single step rather than a flat floor level in the chancel—that is, a single step in front of the altar—is desirable, and gives architectural setting and predetermined position to the site of the altar.

In churches where there is no choir, the depth of the sanctuary can be reduced by a considerable part of the area that would have been required for the choir stalls. There is a tendency under conditions of this character to flatten the plan of the chancel. It is true that not a great deal of space is required. This is one of those instances where use and beauty must stand side by side. We have held that our chancel is the consummate expression of our religious faith. Here beauty must control after usefulness has been developed. In other words, we will have a far handsomer church if we give, instead of a shallow 12 or 14 ft. of depth in the chancel that has no choir, a studied arrangement by skillful planning. Such a design will develop the quiet, depth, richness and interest in our baptistry and altar suitable to the dignity of the church. An additional 8 or 10 ft. over those actually required as minimum space will be a marked help toward achieving

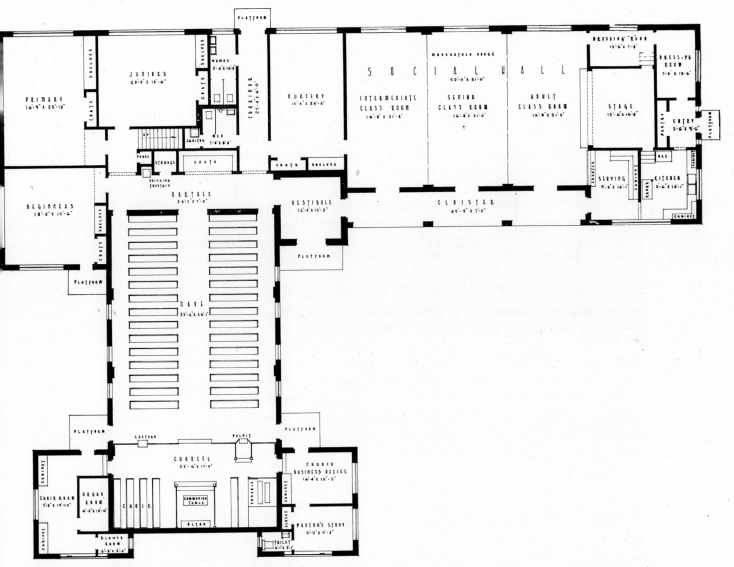

*First Floor Plan for Church and School. Harvin C. Moore, Architect*

classroom capacity equal to the seating capacity of the nave. The manner in which the distribution of children and young people should be arranged depends on the manner of instruction followed by the particular church denomination. There are two rather normal variations. The first follows the gradations of children's age and mental advance and corresponds to the usual twelve grades of public school systems. The second distributes the groups within three assembly levels corresponding to age groups, and then further distributes from the assemblies into relatively small classrooms. There are sound values to each of these methods. The first would appear to be more economical and could develop a plan of wider possible use of the classrooms for additional meeting purposes.

In smaller churches which provide for seatings of about 300 in the nave, still simpler classroom distribution must be accepted; perhaps a minimum of one assembly and six classrooms. This would provide space for one classroom each for kindergarten, beginners, junior, intermediate, senior, and young adult groups. Wherever this is true it will be wise to plan the school in an open and flexible manner which can be easily developed as the numbers increase or the means to provide more generously is attained.

Our classrooms with their assembly or assemblies do not complete the building program of the modern church school. With them must be included the necessary nursery and kindergarten spaces, provision for groups such as the scout organizations, at least modest provision for church guilds, and rooms for adult classes. Still beyond these requirements an efficient modern plant seeks at least one relatively large room, a Hall of Fellowship, suitable for recreational groups of varied nature including occasional use for luncheons or dinners of church members. Important even beyond all of these elements in programming the school is the provision of a minister's study with a conference room and the secretary's office adjacent. Where it is possible, an additional space for the church office separate from that of the secretary proves very desirable. For economy of administration, these offices work well when they are arranged around a small central administration lounge with a church library placed along the walls.

Many plans now in the course of building or in prospect in the immediate future far exceed the provisions outlined here. Among additional facilities is provision for physical exercise, for training and for teams of minor or considerable extent. In some instances such extensive planning will create groups of essentially separate although attached buildings. Just how far duplication on the physical side is practical can best be determined by local conditions. The availability of similar facilities in adjacent city parks or nearby public school groups has a bearing on the advisability of this greater investment within the church plant. Where means is available for the building of a gymnasium and its upkeep by the church, more completeness in the church's work can be expected. In the selection of the site for the new church we should consider perhaps optimistically the number of classrooms and other rooms of parish function and administration which will be required by this church, either now or in the future.

In churches that provide parochial schools through at least the elementary grades it is practical to have the school plant designed in accordance with standards for modern well-studied elementary school buildings. In these instances fewer rooms are attached directly to church building than in the older form of a church school, and the use of these is often limited to church guilds and groups consisting primarily of adults. The parochial school develops as a separate unit. It consists of one or more buildings with suitable recreation areas, and it is important that the general plan be laid out in a manner which will give the maximum convenience to the school for all possible church uses. Flexible or open planning should provide sufficient separation for privacy and protection and for the control of noise.

An orderly sequence in planning our church school is to place the administrative area very close to the church and give it direct contact with the chancel

*Assembly with Small Classrooms for Concurrent Use*

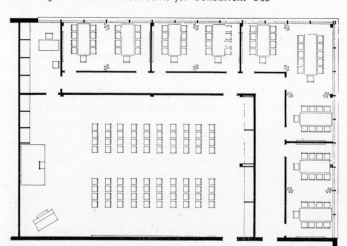

*Chairs arranged for assembly, Second Baptist Church, Houston, Texas. Photo by J. D. Burnette*

end, yet at the same time to allow convenient and direct entrance from the church grounds. This does not mean that the administrative area becomes the principal entrance to the church school. Such entrance should be within the school areas in order to minimize travel distance within the school and to avoid confusion at the administrative zone.

Many clergymen and building committees prefer to locate near the administrative zone rooms used by adult groups, including an adult lounge or meeting room and several relatively large classrooms suitable for meetings of guild members or church club groups. It is usually possible, if we are dealing with a

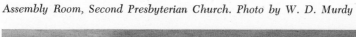

*Assembly Room, Second Presbyterian Church. Photo by W. D. Murdy*

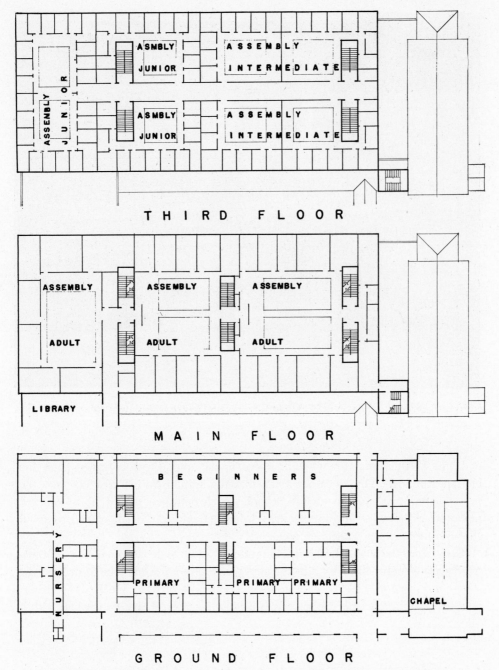

THIRD FLOOR

MAIN FLOOR

GROUND FLOOR

*Diagrammatic Plan of Church School. South Main Baptist Church, Houston, Texas*

*Assembly with Three Classrooms*

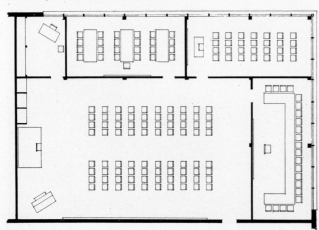

two-story building, to relate these spaces and their areas so that the normal assembly room with large classrooms adjacent may be superimposed above them in a direct structural manner.

Most of the area within our school plan will be occupied by the assembly rooms and classrooms. The number of these will be determined by the total number of children and young people the school is to accommodate. The assembly room is planned for a seating ranging from a minimum of 60 to a sensible maximum of 100. In the diagrammatic plan (page 82), the assembly room is entered from the corridor with the door near the rear of the room. The room is wrapped around with small classrooms. The seating within the assembly provides for 80 children, and the classrooms provide for class groups of eight each. The overall dimensions of the assembly rooms are approximately 28 ft. wide by 48 ft. long. There should be no attempt to crowd the capacity of the room. Generous space is provided for the platform and lectern of the director as well as for the piano by keeping the first row of students from 10 to 11 ft.

*Assembly with Four Classrooms*

*Cloister, South Main Baptist Church. Photos by J. D. Burnette*

away from the front of the room. The aisles to the right and to the left should be approximately 5 ft. wide with the aisle at the center 4 ft. These dimensions are based on four chairs in each row, a total of eight chairs across the room. The plan (page 82) provides for classroom areas slightly greater than 9 by 9 ft. It has proved good practice to build these spaces in units approximately 9 by 18 ft. dividing them at the center by means of multi-fold doors. By this convenience in planning one teacher can instruct two class groups if necessary.

An assembly and classroom unit of this or slightly modified type permits a continuous glass enclosure wall all around the building. This causes each classroom to seem larger and much more attractive. If we are dealing with a one story plan, direct lighting and ventilation into the assembly room is made possible by the lower-ceilinged classroom and the somewhat higher-ceilinged auditorium, with clerestory lighting of the assembly placed above the classroom roof. On the other hand, when we are dealing with a building of more than one

*Cloister, South Main Baptist Church*

story, we will get the best results for quiet within our assembly rooms by means of artificial lighting and modern air-conditioning.

Before considering other diagrams of assembly room arrangements, we should check our plans and the church school schedule to avoid excessive duplication of assembly and classroom areas. This I feel is very important because most of these assembly and classroom areas can be used only on Sunday.

The usual time schedule within the assembly classroom group is one hour. In many instances this is divided as follows: The service of assembly takes the first fifteen minutes of the hour, followed by a thirty minute period of classroom instruction, and a 15 minute closing service. Experiments are constantly being made among the churches, especially the very large churches, to solve the problem of building areas by possible duplication of classes in successive periods. Where this duplication is simply a repetition of assembly service, classroom instruction, and closing service, it sets up a total of a two-hour Sunday school schedule. This schedule does not seem to work out practically for the members of the congregations. The point I wish to make clear is that if the two religious

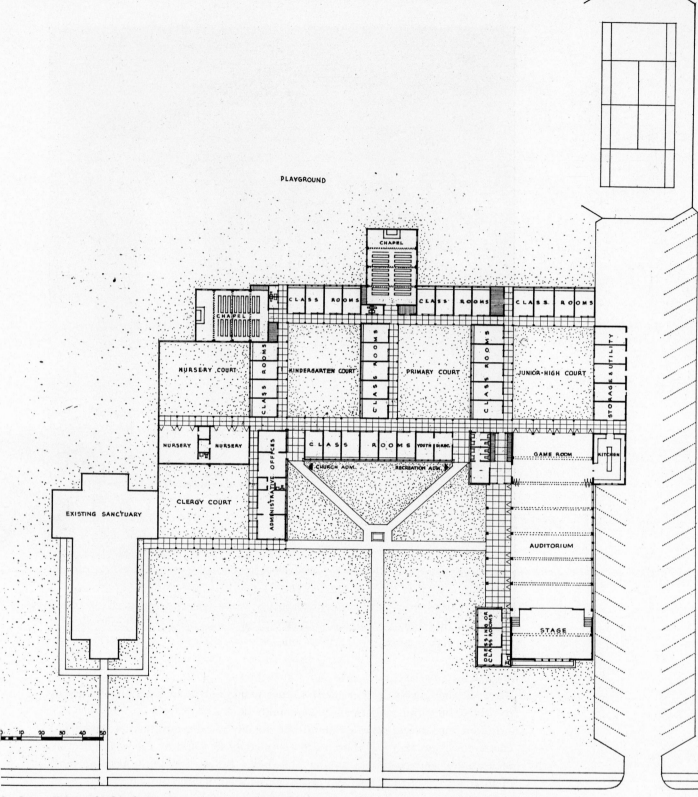

PLAYGROUND

CHAPEL

CLASS ROOMS    CLASS ROOMS    CLASS ROOMS

CHAPEL

NURSERY COURT    CLASS ROOMS    KINDERGARTEN COURT    PRIMARY COURT    CLASS ROOMS    JUNIOR-HIGH COURT    STORAGE & UTILITY

NURSERY    NURSERY    ADMINISTRATIVE OFFICES    CLASS    ROOMS    YOUTH DIREC.    GAME ROOM    KITCHEN

CLERGY COURT    CHURCH ADM.    RECREATION ADM.

EXISTING SANCTUARY    AUDITORIUM

DRESSING OR CLASS ROOMS    STAGE

*St. James Episcopal Church. Dunaway & Jones, Architects*

services in the assembly were combined into a single period of one-half of the hour, and the instruction in the classrooms required the other half-hour, it would be possible, with a properly planned building, to have the instruction in the classroom precede the service in the assembly for one group of students, and the service in the assembly precede the instruction in the classroom for the other half, thereby using the space to the maximum advantage and reducing the building requirements by half. This procedure would schedule the total overall Sunday school period as one hour.

*St. James Episcopal Church.*

An alternate method of using the room would be to start the service for the first group in the assembly and have them pass from the assembly to their classrooms. The assembly would then be occupied by the second group of students, who in turn would proceed to the classrooms at the close of the assembly service, these classrooms having been vacated by the first groups by that time. The duration of assembly period and classroom instruction in each case is still only one half hour, but the rooms would be used over a total of an hour and a half. The diagram (page 84) attempts to meet such a condition. It seems desirable that the classroom zone be provided with more privacy and separation from sound when services in the assembly area and instruction in the classroom area are coincident. There are many possible variants to this solution. The purpose of this design is to gain greater control of the overall cost of the building by the maximum use of the assemblies and classrooms.

A number of the more recent churches have provided still more small classrooms with each assembly room for the beginners age groups of seven to nine years, with instruction groups of six rather than of eight to ten children (page 86). The furniture is smaller and the reduction in classroom size in order to find space for 12 classrooms instead of ten has been worked out very attractively.

In all schools following the assembly and small classroom principle, more teachers are required than in schools where instruction is planned for larger groups corresponding to the age and grade groups of the public schools. Such solutions are indicated by drawings in diagrammatic form on page 86. Here the assemblies provide for three or four public school grades. The classrooms in turn provide area for classes ranging from 25 to 30 in number. It is often true that this later solution is the more economical for churches of small membership where the assemblies can provide for classes on three grade levels. With four classrooms used with each assembly, still further reduction in total area is brought about.

The solution of the plan for the church school of very large parishes is a more difficult problem. In order to continue in a like degree the individual training of the children and young people by keeping the class groups small, complicated building problems develop. I am thinking of churches whose membership passes into the thousands and whose auditoriums provide for possibly from 1200 to 1500. It is not unusual in these great churches to find the membership two or three times the seating capacity of the auditorium of the church, yet often the church school attendance greatly exceeds the number of seatings in the auditorium. In other words, a church whose auditorium seats 1500 persons has a normal attendance in the school far exceeding 2000 young people. Here numbers tend to complicate our planning.

The location of such large churches is often within densely built-up metropolitan areas and therefore an ideal site development is practically impossible. Further land for the church's site must be acquired at very high cost. Consequently, only a modest area will be permitted for the design of the very large church school, and as a result the church school must be built to three or four stories in height and cannot develop around large open courts or gardens such as we desire for smaller churches in residential areas. An example of the planning for a school of such large dimensions and requirements is shown in diagrammatic form on page 86.

On land adjacent to the church shown there has recently been brought to completion the building indicated by the diagram. Fortunately enough land was secured to compose the church school around two sides of a small garden court, with the church on the third side. The front of the court is open to view through an attractive cloister which connects the narthex of the church with the school and with the chapel which is yet to be built as part of the school group.

The first floor of this building is assigned to the nursery groups, the beginners departments, the primary assembly rooms and classrooms. The second floor of the building serves for the adult school. Here are placed three large assembly halls with relatively large classrooms. The third floor is assigned to the junior and young people's departments. Here there are many assembly rooms, each surrounded by a large group of classrooms. The building is practical because it is built as an air conditioned building, correctly lighted with artificial light. This permits assembly areas which are entirely interior rooms, but which have proved entirely efficient.

Where buildings as large and expensive as this church are built, the question immediately develops as to their use throughout the week rather than upon Sunday only. Certainly the larger spaces are brought into use at many intervals throughout the week, but the classroom areas are not sufficiently flexible to permit their use beyond a few hours' service on Sundays. Little by little, as

*Cradle Roll, with Control Desk (Nursery Department). South Main Baptist Church, Houston, Texas*

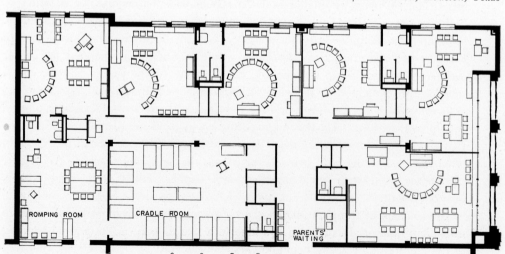

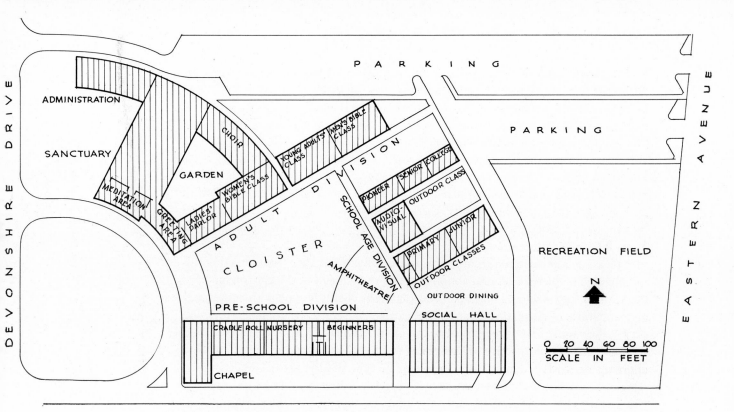

*Westminster Church, Dallas, Texas. White and Prinz, Architects*

modern planning of still more flexible type is accepted, greater usefulness and adaptability of the spaces within the school will be achieved. Year by year, the planning and building of church schools inspires even finer efforts on the part of architects, clergymen and laymen because of the wealth of enduring values such buildings will create and sustain for children, young people, and adults alike.

The degree to which the church chooses to provide for adult instruction within the church school varies greatly. As nearly as I can determine, the adult group comprises the age group above 30. Young people's groups extend from high school graduation to about 30 years. In both of these groups the instruction is advanced and varied, and consequently classroom groups are considerably larger. An effort is occasionally made to set 25 persons as the number for each classroom, but it is more usual to provide for groups of approximately 40 persons. The Fellowship Hall may be used as the assembly area for these adult groups, and if so the classrooms are not directly connected with this hall or with any other assembly. In other schools, the adult assembly room is similar to the usual assembly room in the school, except that it provides seating for from 150 to 200 persons and is arranged with four to six large classrooms wrapped around it. This adult element may be quite different in plan from those which we have previously considered.

The grouping of the assembly and classrooms in this manner has the merit of economy in space, simplicity in construction, and maximum convenience. Other desirable groupings are being developed in a much more open manner than those of earlier churches. The difference is that the designers of these new schools prefer a series of separate classrooms lined along a broad corridor and grouped in sections or departments similar to the grade levels in the public schools. In plans of this type the assembly room may be termed a chapel, and is simply furnished and decorated in a chapel-like manner. Such buildings are made interesting and inviting by the shaping of the plan to form a series of courtyards. A disadvantage, however, is the additional travel and resulting confusion involved in movement from the assembly to the classrooms.

A preceding illustration (page 90) shows a plan of a one story church school on a very beautiful and adequate site, with the administrative wing placed close to the existing church. The plan develops from left to right, having the court of the nursery and beginners groups at the left and the assembly of the primary group at the left rear with its classrooms along an open corridor. Toward the right is the assembly of the intermediate group with its classroom, and finally the right hand side of the plan cares for the senior and young people's groups who are to use the Fellowship Hall for their assembly. Climatic conditions in this area permit an open passage type of corridor. Economy in building cost is being obtained by use of light frame construction throughout some 90 per cent of the area. This frame building is supplemented with attractive brickwork placed at intervals which give pleasing accents to the group. Because it will not be an air conditioned building, the open type corridor and abundant glass at each end of the classrooms have determined the architect's pattern. This plan falls clearly in line with earlier recommendations of adequate site areas and garden courtyards where land areas will permit their use. The development of the church school along the lines indicated by the architect's perspective of this group (page 91) seems necessarily limited to churches of modest dimension. Such a plan can, with slight modification, be developed for a school of two stories with corresponding increase of its capacity. The two-story building would probably waste space and cost more than a compact plan. The one-story form would become unwieldy if required to provide for twice as many children, and control and management would become more difficult. There are reasonable limits within which the one or two story groupings become restricted.

In plans where larger requirements for numbers in the intermediate and secondary groups exist and the church has secured large and generous site areas, one and two-story groupings are being developed. Such plans are either grouped around courts or arranged in a radiating manner which avoids undue concentration of school elements within a single building. An extended plan

*Beginners' Romping Room. South Main Baptist Church, Houston, Texas. Photo by J. D. Burnette*

of this character is shown on page 93. The plan extends far beyond the usual number of units and opens for our thinking a vista which may become desirable in planning churches to be built in the future.

*St. Rose of Lima School, Houston, Texas. Photo by Ulric Meisel*

*Kindergarten, Sinai Temple, Chicago. Photo by Hedrich Blessing*

*Cribs in Nursery Department. Central Church of Christ. Photo by Shoemake-Stiles*

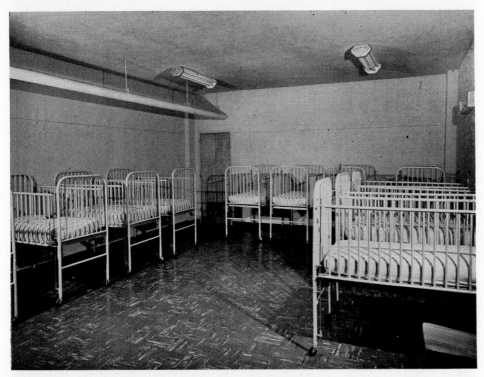

*Cribs in Nursery Department. South Main Baptist Church. Photo by J. D. Burnette*

Provision for other functions so necessary within the school will be referred to in next chapter. By such functions I refer to the nursery department (which includes the cradle groups and those of kindergarten and pre-kindergarten ages), those sections of the school which provide for the larger social meetings, lectures, and dinners in a Fellowship Hall, and the section for offices of the administration.

The nursery department of a modern church school attracts great interest among the laymen. It pleasantly accents the completeness of the school. This department generally provides for the care of children up to and through their third year. Its minimum space requirement can be limited to a cradle room, with suitable equipment, and a romping room. With this minimum nursery area there should be placed at least one large classroom equipped along the lines suitable for beginners groups—a room of essentially pre-kindergarten nature. In certain churches these two elements have been grouped into a single department with

*Beginners' Room. South Main Baptist Church, Houston, Texas. Photo by J. D. Burnette*

a plan so organized that it works efficiently, and yet has a degree of isolation. The diagram, on page 92, is from a very recent work. The reader will note that the department is entered through a generous reception area presided over by a teacher at a control desk, where parents bring and return for their children. It provides comfortable seating for parents waiting for their children to be brought from the respective nursery or beginners rooms.

The more modern solutions reflect widely differing local habits and customs. There are wide variations, for example in capacities required in the nursery section. The cradle room, while not at all new in church school planning, will appear very large in one plan and quite restricted in another, even though adequate means were at hand to equip them as either large or small areas. The minimum provision should allow for at least six beds. One church with nearly a generation of continuous cradle room experience decided to limit the number of beds to 20. The school plant provided for over 1200 people, and the church membership exceeded 2000. In another example, 24 beds were in weekly use in a school of only 800 and a church seating 1000. In each of the above cases the cradle room capacities seem to be exactly what those particular churches need. Just how far post-war conditions and other social changes may modify previous experience is impossible to say. I feel that there is a growing understanding regarding the usefulness and convenience of the entire nursery area, which tends to increase the memberships of this department. Therefore, it is better to over-plan slightly than to minimize the areas assigned.

The cradle room shown on page 96 uses the larger and higher type of child's bed. These slightly increase the required dimensions of the room. Beds of this type have proved more convenient and practical for the women who supervise and care for the infants entrusted to this area. The purpose of the room is essentially that of rest and feeding. No effort is made to decorate the walls or other objects. The equipment is neat, orderly and of clean-cut modern design. A small sink, a small refrigerator, and cabinet storage space are included, and the room requires a small toilet area adjacent. Extremely small size fixtures should be used. In addition to the equipment mentioned, it is customary to install sterilizing lamp equipment in the nursery area as a further health protection. This practice has become so general that it should be considered part of the required furnishing.

Adjacent to the cradle room is the romping room (page 94) which requires no special equipment but must provide space for actual play with a variety of toys. Those parents who have availed themselves of these church school facilities for very young children are very nearly unanimous in their praise and satisfaction. Beyond the actual convenience they find a definite educational value for their children in the weekly association with other infants in this room.

Beginners classrooms require greater care of furniture and the manner in which it is placed, and permit more simple but more decorative interest than is necessary in the classrooms of either the primary or intermediate departments. Wherever possible the outlook from these kindergarten areas should include attractive lawns, trees and flowers. The glass area can be extensive. Such a room as shown on page 97, indicates the position of furniture and equipment as it is normally placed. This same room is also shown in photograph, page 94. Attention is called to the use of sunken metal picture moulds around all of the plastered walls. The mould is placed at a height 7 ft. from the floor. It is convenient for hanging the small black board, framed or unframed pictures, drawings, and other illustrations which by frequent change provide continual active interest within the room. This type of sunken mould was used throughout all of the assembly rooms and the larger classrooms of the building.

All classroom-assembly groups as well as nursery groups and beginners groups within the school are necessarily served by corridors. In warm climates the small one-story school can be developed along the lines of open circulation so widely used in modern public schools in similar localities. In general, however, the enclosed corridor remains the means of circulation in the church school. As such, it receives the normal use and abuse characteristic of school corridors. Among the more attractive solutions in recent schools have been corridor walls of light grey-pink brick laid with flush joints and extending from floor to ceiling. Still more colorful solutions have used structural glazed tile as the material for the corridor walls. With a glaze of light sea-green tone, the tile corridor seems even more attractive than the brick, and should require considerably less upkeep.

There is no occasion for the corridor ceiling to exceed 8 ft. in height. This is a very desirable height in buildings which have assembly rooms with ceilings of 9 ft. 6 in. to 10 ft. on one or both sides of the corridor. Since the dimensions of the corridor area are smaller than those of the assembly rooms, ceiling heights of 8 ft. in the corridors and 10 ft. in the assemblies are in good proportion. This arrangement also permits the installation of ventilating ducts above the corridor with direct outlet through the corridor walls into the assembly areas.

The architect and the building committee should select attractive colors for the entire school area. Color is as important in classrooms for adults as in classrooms for children. In addition to the maximum of daylight, generous uniform artificial lighting should prevail. Under these conditions the walls should be of light tones but of varied colors, since the school becomes much more cheerful if much repetition of a single color is avoided (page 97). Further variation can be gained by using a different color of deeper tone for the wall at the rostrum end of an assembly room, or the instructor's end of a large classroom.

In many instances too little thought has been given to interesting floor color. Materials such as asphalt tile or rubber tile are particularly suited to church school floors, and by careful choice among the wide range of colors available in these materials, delightful rooms can be produced. It is amazing how very stimulating the beginners and primary areas become with floors of the clearer reds and the deeper blues. The architect should make an effort to go beyond his more conservative tastes and work for color in all of the church school rooms, rather than be satisfied with pleasant variations of greys so usual in earlier work.

No room can show its best possible artistic development unless care and good judgment are exercised in the choice of its furnishings as well as its decorations.

*Lecture Lounge, Fondren Library, Rice Institute, Houston, Texas. Staub and Rather, Architects; W. W. Watkin Consulting Architect. Photos by Burt Moritz*

In this respect the equipment within public school classrooms still seems to fall far short when compared with the better modern furnishings chosen by capable architects for use in church school rooms. In general these architects are to be commended for their choice of light-colored finishes. Woods of very light natural color or darker woods purposely bleached to much lighter tones add a real freshness to the room. There is little occasion for color combinations in the relatively simple pieces of furniture necessary for either the classrooms or the assemblies. The furniture of public school buildings has long tended to relatively dark woods made darker by the finishes placed on them. This furniture after its newness disappeared, became increasingly dull. The church school is indeed a very opportune place to build up consciousness of colorful surroundings in the mind of a growing child.

Our plan carries us further to rooms of still more specialized interest. One of these is relatively recent in its appearance within the church school: we will call it the visual aid library. Every assembly room and every large classroom throughout the school should be equipped with electric outlets conveniently placed and of adequate voltage for use of both simple projectors and projectors with sound equipment. It is impractical and unnecessary to supply individual pieces of this equipment for each classroom, or even each assembly room. Their use is not necessarily simultaneous or coincident. A room should be provided in which the projectors may be stored in an orderly manner with proper designation to each piece of equipment. The size of the room will vary with the size of the school, but a room 14 ft. wide by 18 to 20 ft. long will normally serve quite well even for a large school (page 98).

Cabinets for the storage of lantern slides and short films complete the equipment required. Where the department of visual aids is under the direction of a churchman experienced in its use, the material available tends to increase

*Fondren Library Lounge converted into a small lecture hall*

constantly without great expenditure. Occasional interesting films of entertainment or educational merit and length are secured with a scheduled program of circulation. This brings still more activity to the church school throughout the week days. Such films are shown either in the larger assembly rooms, or (possibly more appropriately) in the fellowship hall.

The mention of the fellowship hall carries us to still further study of one of the important specialized rooms of our church school. Here still greater diversity of opinion prevails. This is primarily due to the persistent desire which still exists among some building committees that the large hall shall serve every possible purpose including physical exercise. In a great majority of cases, church committees are quite willing for the fellowship hall to serve any consistent variety of purposes, provided these purposes are not necessarily handicapped by design for physical exercise. The sensible position to take is that the fellowship hall should be a thoroughly modern church room as attractive in every degree as we can afford to make it. To this end we declare that it should not be made a hybrid gymnasium. If a gymnasium is necessary, it should be built as such and in no way confused with the fellowship hall.

We should not exaggerate the capacity of the hall which we have planned. It is not necessary to build another auditorium reaching or approaching the dimensions of our church. The fellowship hall invites very frequent use by groups of varying age levels and interests. For a church whose nave seats 500 people, a fellowship hall should be large enough to serve comfortably a group ranging from 125 to 150 at a church dinner. Consequently it would comfortably seat some 250 or more for an entertainment or lecture.

Fellowship halls in churches of the past generation have usually appeared very barren. They were either nearly empty, or filled with folding chairs which added no interest to the room. Instead, the hall should be an attractive lounging

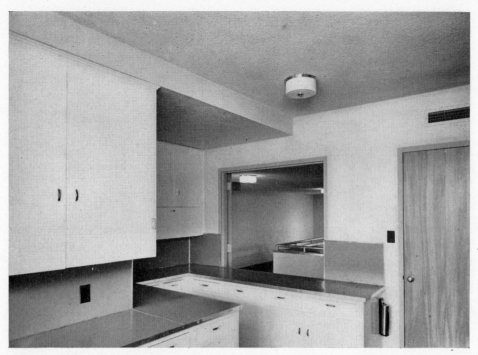

*Auxiliary Kitchen, Second Presbyterian Church, showing opening for cafeteria service*

room for the church members. It is perfectly practical to furnish such a room adequately in pieces well grouped and well chosen for their design, and so create a useful social unit less formal and less uniform than the elements of the school proper. Countless examples are to be found in splendidly designed tennis clubs, small country clubs, etc. which provide an attractive dining room or an attractive space for lectures. By similarly designing the fellowship hall we can bring to the church school a thoroughly modern social and scientific solution of cultural value. The accompanying illustrations (pages 100, 101) are not from a fellowship hall, but rather from a hall termed a "lecture lounge." This hall is one of the public rooms in the new Fondren Library, The Rice Institute, Houston. The first photograph shows the room in its regular lounge-like setting with the furniture in almost its customary position. The dimensions of the room are some 37 by 65 ft. and it is attractively furnished. Because its acoustical qualities as a live room were carefully studied, it is possible for a speaker to address informally a group seated at the usual furniture groupings scattered throughout the room. The speaker does not have to raise his voice above that of usual conversation level, and no mechanical amplification is necessary. The second photograph shows the use of this room when a larger number of persons attends a formal lecture. Little movement of lounge furniture from its normal position is necessary. One hundred and fifty additional seatings can be brought in. These chairs have light aluminum frames with canvas backs and seats, and are stored in a nearby room.

Careful designing should provide flexibility in the use of the fellowship hall, which could serve the needs of the church better than it has in the past. It should provide for use as well as beauty. The hall may be designed to serve small gatherings such as teas or receptions, large formal or informal lectures and a variety of entertainment with music or movies; and certainly should have a floor suitable for dancing. It is my opinion that the fellowship hall is a fertile field for the imagination of architects, clergymen, and laymen. Here they may seek to achieve maximum beauty and usefulness with all the attributes of graciousness.

*Stove and counters, Auxiliary Kitchen. Second Presbyterian Church, Houston, Texas*

In order that the fellowship hall may develop efficiently all of its possibilities, it is particularly important that auxiliary rooms be properly related to it. This is especially true if the hall is reached from the corridors of the school. It should also be served by a direct entrance from the church grounds. On reaching this entrance we should enter an attractive vestibule or foyer of modest dimension.

*Small Kitchen. Photos by J. D. Burnette*

*Library, South Main Baptist Church, Houston, Texas. Calhoun & Tungate, Architects; Jackson & Dill, Associates. Photo by J. D. Burnette*

*Reception Room and Office, South Main Baptist Church. Photo by J. D. Burnette*

It is wise to provide direct entrance to this foyer from the corridor of the school as well. Adequate coat rooms, powder rooms and control desk are necessary. The usual conveniences within the school will not be suitable for the use of the fellowship hall.

The fellowship hall requires a well-arranged modern kitchen and pantry area in order to serve efficiently as a dining hall. This element of the plan is often unnecessarily large. Convenience is far more fundamental than elaboration and multiplication of equipment. The meals are usually of a relatively simple nature and are served by women members of the church. The architect should try to

*Sunday School Library, Sinai Temple, Chicago. Photo by Hedrich-Blessing*

*Small Parlor, Central Presbyterian Church, Houston, Texas. Lloyd L. Morgan, Architect. Photo by W. C. Murdy*

reach a solution which reduces the laborious aspect of this service. The kitchen shown above on pages 102 and 103 is a modern installation in a recently built church. It can serve more than a usual number at dinners. It was planned for complete preparation of food for the entire meal. In many instances it is practical to plan for a less complete kitchen because heavier foods are prepared else-

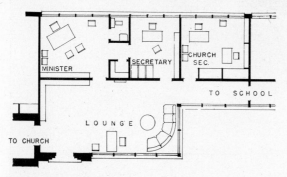

*Administration Department
for Small Church*

where and delivered to the steam tables of the kitchen. Here, as in all other aspects of the modern school, we have a right to expect that the equipment selected is in all respects practical and efficient. It is impossible to meet this required service if the kitchen is designed only as a modern domestic kitchen. Such areas and equipment are inadequate, and place a very heavy burden on the women who attempt to use them for the preparation of church dinners. The area should be at least three times the size of a large home kitchen and pantry area, and serving tables, with generous circulation around them, should occupy at least one-half of the total area.

While considering food service, it is well to note that the more modern schools include small food service areas in locations other than the fellowship hall. One of these has been mentioned in connection with the cradle room. A simple modern unit kitchen is also useful in the beginners department. A single piece of equipment providing a small amount of refrigerated storage space and burner space with drawers for utensils is often adequate if used in connection with small storage cabinets and a sink. An alcove some 9 ft. square will accommodate this equipment, and it can be attractively shut off by means of a multifold door.

At least one other area within the school should have similar equipment. This is the young people's department, where social meetings of 30 or 40 people are frequently held in the late afternoon or evening hours. Young people will use such an area more frequently and more conveniently if it is so equipped, and will seldom require the fellowship hall for their meetings. A wider program of church activities will be possible if the fellowship hall can be in use at the same hours as the young people's department. A small kitchen following somewhat the lines suggested here is shown on page 103.

*Administration Department
for Large Church*

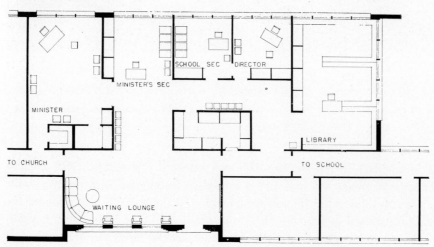

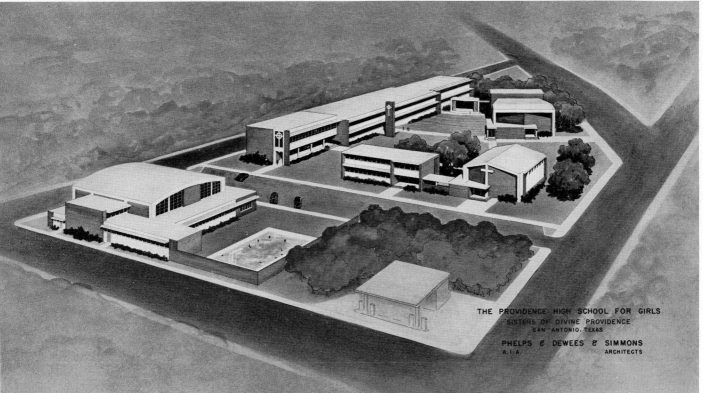

*Parochial High School, San Antonio, Texas. Phelps, Dewees and Simmons, Architects*

It has been my purpose to advise against duplication within the school wherever possible. I feel that there should be considerable effort to bring to maximum use the modern facilities that the church has been able to build. Time scheduling and other intelligent direction will help to make maximum use of the church building. Often the committees, urged by practical church members, are called upon to extend their basic plan requirements by the addition of special rooms for this or that purpose. Occasionally a social room smaller than the fellowship hall will seem advisable. This room should have the qualities we have described

*Sunday School Lobby, Sinai Temple, Chicago. Friedman, Alschuler and Sincere, Architects. Photo by Hedrich-Blessing*

for the fellowship hall, but should provide for the social meetings of less than 100 persons, and would not be used for so many varied purposes. It can be more formal, and, especially if given by a single donor as a memorial room, more richly decorated (page 105). Here again we would have occasion for the very small efficient kitchen to meet such requirements as those of social teas. A room of this character by custom seems to be most used for women's gatherings and church clubs. It serves their purposes well, and in doing so serves the church. However, the more modern church plants have ceased to overlook the men of the congregation. In fact, in some of the most popular and growing parishes the constant interest seems to be sustained because a desirable social room for men has been provided.

Such a room will vary in accordance with the size of the parish, and in no circumstances needs to be a large room. It should be adequate to serve efficiently for Bible classes of 40 to 60 men. It should, however, be arranged with lounge furniture adequate to care for a score of persons. If so designed it does not appear cluttered with folding chairs at times when they are not needed, nor does it appear empty at other times. The men's social room should have a direct entrance from the exterior, because men do not enjoy making their way through corridors filled with children of primary or beginners age. Two useful auxiliaries are appropriate to this area. One is proximity to a small kitchen or kitchen alcove from which it is possible to provide at least coffee and doughnuts. The other, which is less necessary but very useful, is a small darkroom alcove fitted with a small sink and lighting suitable for photographic work. Members of the clergy have informed me that where adequate space for men was provided even in the most modest manner, the men have initiated efforts to secure additional furniture and equipment throughout the entire school, and the results have been very gratifying.

Completing our survey of the necessary elements within the school plan, we return to the administration department. We have suggested that this department should have direct contact with the church as well as with the church school. Its minimum requirements constitute the office or study of the minister, a room for his secretary, a room for the church office or church secretary, an office for the

*St. Rose of Lima School, Houston, Texas. Donald Barthelme & Associates, Architects*

director of the church school, and a small waiting room and library. If we visit churches built as much as a generation ago, we will be amazed at the inconvenience and confusion which have accumulated in the limited area provided for this most active work. The offices and adjacent corridors are often littered with unseemly storage equipment and with dusty material that is not stored. The continuity and extent of work done in this area of the church is amazing. That it is done as efficiently as it is is a high credit to the energy of the clergy and their usually limited number of assistants.

The clerical work done within this area requires suitable space for mimeograph machines, addressograph machines, dictaphones, etc., and adequate storage for church pamphlets and literature, as well as cabinets for the supplies for each of these services. The number of secretaries will vary with the activities of the particular parish. The church office should be as comfortable as the office of a single business executive, and should have a vault for keeping records and a safe within the vault. The office of the director of the church school is often entirely overlooked. In a large school this office should be adequate for at least two or three desks, and serve as a conference room for small groups of teachers.

The plan works to the best advantage if the study of the minister is placed, as seems most sensible, at the end of the administrative area which is nearest to the church. We may have considered the choir room, as it truly is, part of the church plant rather than the school plant, but still it is frequently placed immediately next to the minister's study on this side adjoining the church. Near the choir room it is desirable to have at least a small office or private space for the organist, provided with generous cabinets for the storage of music.

When such a department as we have described for the administration of the church and the church school is planned in an attractive manner and has direct access from the church school, we tend to build up a good working plan. If when we enter from the church or from the church school grounds we come into a well-designed waiting room attractively decorated and well furnished, we at once have greater respect for the practical working officers of our church. I recently visited the administration section of a very modern church building

*St. Gregory School, St. Louis, Missouri. Joseph Murphy, Architect. Photo by Robert Frei*

in which all of these provisions except that of the waiting room had been provided. It lacked the final touch that would have given it conviction, although its clerical areas were considerably finer than those I have outlined. Our survey has been sufficiently extended for us to realize the great usefulness and completeness of the modern church school. However, the fact that we contemplate designing and building a church plant which will serve all of these purposes should inspire still further practical inquiry. The church school should acquire greater and more continuous usefulness. One such outlet is the use mentioned earlier of a number of the church school rooms for daily instruction during the summer period when the public schools are closed. We find an occasional church scheduling use of classrooms and assembly rooms at the nursery and beginners levels throughout the year. This important service is rendered as a convenience to employed parents. Every step which results from good designing and good building which make possible greater usefulness of the church plant leads to a stronger and more sincere civilization.

It becomes more evident as we visualize the requirements of the church school that they approach or tend to approach the building forms which have evolved with amazing attractiveness in the field of the elementary schools. Possibly it is within the design range of the church school that the traditional forms of church building have shown themselves lacking. I recently had occasion to examine the perspective drawings of several proposed church groups which reflected good planning and good composition in mass. Unfortunately, however, the modern designs carried the scale relationship of window openings as related to each other in traditional design. That is, in comparison with the relatively large window openings of the church, the school windows were deliberately reduced. Such designing would result in inadequately lighted classrooms and assembly rooms, and would fail to create the attractiveness which is essential to these classroom areas. We must accept walls of glass as appropriate throughout our classroom areas.

Wherever we are able to confine our church school to one story, the design solution is relatively simple. Large if not continuous glass areas, suitably shaded by an overhanging roof, fit very well into the perspective of the church group. The monotony of continuous glass is easily overcome by some interesting play

*Youth Building, Travis Park*
*Methodist Church, San Antonio, Texas*
*Henry Steinborner, Architect*
*Photo by Harvey Patteson & Son*

of masonry solids at occasional locations. The plan forms of the school adapt themselves to such composition.

We gain a clear picture of a design containing large useful glass areas, yet interrupted appropriately with adequate masonry masses which create interest and avoid monotony in the drawing of the parochial high school on page 107.

*Church School, Second Baptist Church, Houston, Texas. Wirtz, Calhoun & Tungate, Architects. Photo by J. D. Burnette*

The school is now in course of building and the perspective shows the school room section of this large parochial plant. We should expect to find more and more classrooms employing large glass areas.

The problem of glass areas and their solution in the overall design of the church school is more difficult when the school is a two- or three-story rather than a one-story building. Unless there is a noticeable distinction between the forms used on the first floor and those used on the second floor, the designs approach monotony despite their practical usefulness (page 110). Wherever possible, either the masking of the class areas with appropriate shadow throughout the first floor level or the shadowing of the glass areas of the second floor level by means of an overhanging roof should be accepted. In this manner a degree of interest will be added in a very attractive way.

Still larger schools, requiring more than two stories, can quite readily accept the more modern design values of the larger public schools. However, the church school plant of more than two stories is usually the outcome of limited site conditions such as prevail in metropolitan neighborhoods. It is not usually a design developed as part of an entirely new church plant, but the result of the necessity for greater facilities in connection with a large existing plant. In these cases the conflict with architectures of traditional type is to be expected. The best results will be attained by the use of building materials similar to those of the church buildings, retaining in the new church school a character acceptable and comfortable within its environment, yet showing greater cleanliness of form and larger areas of glass, with willingness to declare the school-like purpose of the building. Such an example is shown on this page. A restraint which is in fitting relation to the classic tradition of the church group is evident in the design of this school. Vast glass areas were less essential and possibly less desirable due to a location surrounded by heavy traffic and considerable

**112**

noise.   Comfort and quiet were attained by means of air conditioning throughout the entire plant.

Even amidst traffic conditions of nearly maximum degree, it is possible to attain quiet and convenience necessary for church school services if we avail ourselves of modern scientific solution.   It is also possible to design in a manner which will pass distinctly beyond the commercial aspect of such locations.   An example of rather startling interest has been erected for the Travis Park Methodist Church of San Antonio (page 111).   This recently completed work represents the first stage in the remodeling and rebuilding of a very large city church which is located on a limited site surrounded by constant traffic.

The more basic elements of the exterior design of the church and the church school are recorded in a later chapter where it is appropriate to consider the new churches and the new church schools as they are being planned in areas providing adequate sites and desirable environments.

# WALLS AND TOWERS

Churches have too often been designed entirely for their conspicuousness. A quieter and more sensitive approach would have eliminated many of the inferior forms and ornaments characteristic of church building in the last generation. The process of placing value and importance where it truly belongs is one which requires a critical as well as a reverent attitude on the part of the committee and architect.

Our modern churches should be dignified, colorful, and restrained, but suitable to the residential communities in which they are built. Such an approach will discard elaborate details where they may be meaningless and out of place.

Traditional parish churches were relatively quiet, solidly built, but simple masses. Without any direct effort toward tradition, the good sense which suggested such sturdy, simple forms as fitting to the church could well carry its full meaning into our church buildings of today.

Likewise, churches during the Middle Ages placed priority of mass in the church itself and secondary importance of mass to attendant buildings, whether they serve as church school, rectory or for other church purposes. This consistency in placing first things first could well guide our builders of today.

From the churches of long tradition we have learned the meaning of structural soundness, which expressed a sense of permanence. Lest in modern building we move too readliy to accept the temporary, it is well that we think of our church as permanent and lasting, and try to design accordingly with all the means that we have at hand.

Some of our modern churches seek novel form and tend toward a dramatic mass with the religious purpose marked by the placing of a cross against the exterior wall. Bareness that tends to be repelling rather than inviting is frequently seen. This is not unnatural when so persistent an effort has been made to discard traditional form and to seek an intriguing freshness of composition. Examples of such churches are scattered far apart over the nation. They do not relate themselves to public understanding, and therefore they are but the beginning of an evolution which will eventually achieve restraint with beauty and a delightful fitness of the church building to its environment. We should be fair in saying that the skill and the ability of the architects is present and equal to the test. The task is an arduous one. Their finest effort and their most serious work will be required to produce an evolution that is convincing. I see no reason in willful efforts to design a church that will not look like a church. The tremendous variety of modern form throughout commercial, industrial, and educa-

*Church of the Epiphany, New York City. Wyeth & King and Eugene Mason, Associated Architects. Photo by Louis H. Dreyer*

tional work has rapidly created many buildings, dispersed throughout the entire country, from which the citizens of nearly every large city may decide which seem good and which seem bad. The consensus of such opinion is usually right. It accepts novel designs for commercial and amusement building, more staid and massive forms in public building, and a more colorful, graceful and welcoming architecture throughout its residential areas. Progress in each of these fields is cumulative, coming within the understanding and acceptance of our people. We can look forward with conviction, knowing that when our modern churches demand the dignity, the refinement, and the graceful gentleness to be expected of the church, their forms will express less of the artificial, dramatic design and much more of serious, serene solution.

In the more recent work of those offices whose churches held to traditional form there has developed an understanding of simplicity and an expression of fine solidity. We could expect this to be the evolution of architects who, though

*Chancel Window, St. Ann's Church, Normandy, Missouri. Emil Frei, Designer. Full daylight, with no interior lighting*

well-versed in the forms of older civilizations, know that for modern design these characteristics are far more important than any traditional detail. In fact, it was the historic detail which so definitely dated the work of outstanding offices, and separated their buildings from the daily habit and custom of our people. Medieval detail, at its best, was unequalled even by the works of Greece. It brought to completeness the fine work of the Gothic period. This could not justify its reproduction four or five hundred years later on the streets of New York, Chicago, or San Francisco. It has taken us two generations to understand this clearly. As a result, we can expect from the finer artists who have sentiment and tradition richly wrought within their spirit of design, a mastery that will express the emotional values of the church without a great deal of detail. The detail they give us will be of our own age and pattern.

We must recover the high emotional values of the church. The conflicting philosophies, and the conflicting standards of governments, and of people, have caused confusion and unrest. The church as an institution has represented the values of life and behavior and worthwhile democracy. To seek to build our churches with the sense of function only, in the lesser standard of usefulness, is to endanger rather than to strengthen the great institution of the church. The exterior of our church creates our first impression of its purpose. Its work and services come from within. No futile forms should be used to confuse this truth. The impression we build as we design our walls and roofs, should be a sincere and gracious embodiment of the shelter for the shrine within.

The use of large glass areas appearing in recent designs can become inappropriate. Sometimes this large area occupies the entire space of the sanctuary

*Chancel Window, St. Ann's Church, shown with interior lighting*

wall behind the high altar. The glass is often treated as though essentially transparent and gives vistas upon gardens or forests. No matter how beautiful these gardens or forests, the result will be a distraction which is in opposition to the essential service about the altar. In other instances, the field of glass has been thought of as a tapestry in glass, a rich colorful form with possible splendid meaning. When the glass can be created with skill and artistry fully commensurate with the religious meaning sought, it is worth trying, as is being done in the window by Emil Frei at St. Ann's Church in St. Louis above.

Large fields of glass have been thought of not only as a solution of the wall of the sanctuary, but also as solutions for walls to the right or to the left of the nave, and even the entire front of the building. As we noted in connection with the interior of the church, there is a real opportunity to use considerable areas of glass in the side walls, provided they are aisle walls and do not open directly into the pew space of the nave. The lighting through the width of the aisle could be very good. It might occur on one side of the church and not on the other, particularly if there is a garden court in the church school group. All confusing vistas such as the passing of people or traffic which could be seen through such glass areas by the congregation must be avoided.

Finally, as to making the front of the church a field of glass, this seems to be playing with modern material simply because we have it. It is not desirable for the clergy at the chancel to look at a vast field of glass behind their congregation, nor for the congregation to have behind them, as it were, an open-ended church, lacking the normal enclosing character of a welcoming interior. In my opinion we could well be firm, restrained, and sensible as to the use of glass on the western

**117**

*Parker Memorial Methodist Church, Houston, Texas. Herman Lloyd, Architect. Photo by Paul Dorsey*

or entrance end of our nave. Seldom was even the much smaller stained-glass window over the entrance doorway very helpful or useful as viewed from the interior. Designers should recognize the acoustical problems which become rapidly intensified as we develop large areas of glass. It is needless to complicate the acoustics deliberately.

Viewing the entire mass composition of the exterior of our church, we find more change from tradition than we find within the church. For instance, in the new Methodist Church of Midland, Mich. by Alden Dow, Architect, the group forms a composition with courts and gardens beginning just beyond the walls of the chapel. The chapel is conveniently located at the front of the church, and is entered from the vestibule which gives access to the church itself. The arrangement causes a broader and lower mass than is usual at the church front. Its forms are entirely modern and seem to promise great beauty. The entrance is expressed in a generous, open manner. As we view the church from the gardens, a degree of openness between the nave and the garden is sensitively arranged so as to create an attractive vista. This rather open treatment toward the garden is flanked by solid masses of the chapel at the front and the chancel at the rear, repeating a motif widely favored in good modern composition. Elsewhere the

St. Ann's Catholic Church, San Antonio, Texas. Julian and White, Architects. Photo by Harvey Patteson & Son

St. Matthew's Methodist Church, Houston, Texas. Harvin Moore, Architect. Photo by Emily Charton

design continues the use of modern materials in a modern manner with low walls, well-handled horizontals, and suitable landscape treatment.

Our impression of a design of this character is that it has sought no self-conscious ostentation. We feel that the forms are appropriate to their use, but are refined rather than crude, and therefore suitable to church architecture. This is a distinction we must keep constantly in mind.

With the modern work of Dow, one might place the almost equally modern solution of the Church of the Epiphany in New York City as shown on page 115. Here we find a North European influence. The brickwork is very attractive, very solid in appearance and free from ornament. This is a small building, yet it carries dignity in the large tower form topped with its steeply pointed roof. The tower form is, in truth, the elevated, lofty chancel of the church. The windows in the upper level of the tower open directly into the chancel, high above the floor. This permits walls of great simplicity, unbroken by openings. It also permits a lofty dorsal, of beautiful color, as a hanging immediately behind the altar. The lighting is more abundant than in the nave, and therefore further accents the interest and importance of the chancel. These useful elements of design are reflected in the exterior in a direct and appropriate manner. There are those who may say that this is scarcely what we mean when we say modern design. I differ with them. The shape, size and number of window openings or other voids created in the wall surfaces of a church, do not necessarily have to be divorced from all historic proportion and grouped in a totally unique way to produce a building which may be termed modern. If we are in favor of building more and more modern churches for use and for beauty, we will appreciate skills and good taste that are apparent in the exterior of this small Church of the Epiphany.

We cannot leave the discussion of the exterior of the church without at least mentioning the term architectural style. Style may be but a picture from history, essentially sterile or stagnant. In a greater sense it may be the inspiration and guide to further and more modern forms of beautiful building. In the field of church building today, it is still true that the favorite form continues the traditions of the meeting-house building which found its inception in America. Its style was derived from the churches of Wren, Gibbs and Jones in England. The form has persisted throughout our history and is typified by the charm of

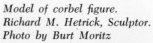
*Model of corbel figure.*
*Richard M. Hetrick, Sculptor.*
*Photo by Burt Moritz*

*First Baptist Church, Longview, Texas. Wilson, Morris and Crain, Architects*

the meeting houses of New England and the churches throughout Virginia. It is a simple plan form easily adaptable to present-day customs. It continues in high favor. The points of interest, however, for us as architects are not the willful discard of an appropriate useful scheme, but rather the search for skills which permit us to avoid imitation. We have, therefore, in this particular stylistic type, a greater opportunity to achieve a crispness and a freshness which will be appropriate to a modern church.

The quiet dignity of both the mass and the detail in well-designed churches of Colonial tradition still justifies the favor with which they are held by many of the clergy and laymen. While this type of exterior treatment does not invite excessive modernizing, still very pleasing and very simple solutions have been developed. An example of this nature is the Parker Memorial Methodist Church of Houston (page 118). It seems to have all of the simpleness of form that was characteristic of the Colonial types, yet it is definitely a modern design.

In contrast to such examples of modernism to which there still clings a degree of the traditional, we find forms which are very novel. A design of this nature has recently been completed in St. Ann's Catholic Church of San Antonio, Tex., (page 119). The west front is decorated with a glazed grill, the pattern of which continues around the entrance with a feeling of openness and welcome. This is a small parish church and the scale has been kept very modest. Many of the most modern works represent churches of small scale.

Among the smaller churches attractive buildings have appeared which are entirely of wood. Naturally the wooden church suggests extreme simplicity and is best when it adheres to such simpleness.

Combinations of wood with brick have been developed with directness and simplicity (page 119). The choice of wood in these smaller churches or chapels has been controlled by efforts at economy, but the degree of economy reached by such a choice has not been sufficient to popularize church buildings of wood rather than masonry. Very simple walls of brick are popular because they can express dignity and still be inexpensive.

**121**

*Conventual Church of St. Mary and St. John. Cambri dge, Massachusetts. Cram and Ferguson, Architects. Photo by Haskell*

Many of the churches built of wood rather than masonry appeared immediately following the close of World War II, or were built during the war. The economies of post-war building have made use of relatively low cost materials and very plain and inexpensive patterns. There has been a tendency to exaggerate the permanent meaning of these simple designs rather than to state their reason frankly. We should compliment those who did creditable work with the simplest of materials and at a minimum of expense, but we should certainly continue to recognize that the church has higher purpose and more lasting greatness which demands more serious and more sturdy architectural work.

There has been a recovery of this meaning in the churches now in course of building or now in course of design. The First Baptist Church of Longview, Tex. (page 121) shows the simplicity of sturdy brickwork. The building is not small, nor is there any trace of makeshift. The mass is as simple as that of the medieval period; but the forms are very modern. The tremendous masonry solids at the west front, with the vertical pylons extending from the ground to the roof, recall the qualities of ancient building.

This church design accents the vertical qualities of the west front by means of shafts centered between the great pylons. The corbeled figures of angels im-

*Cranbrook Episcopal Church, Cranbrook, Michigan. Bertram G. Goodhue and Associates, Architects. Photo by Harvey Croze*

mediately above the large doors, are designed to conform to the slender proportions (page 120), and are of heroic size. The sculptor is Richard M. Hetrick. The entire effect of this crisply modern treatment of the west front is a recovery of good scale, the discarding of meagre dimensions, and an acceptance of adequate mass. These are, indeed, appropriate qualities for the modern church.

Post-war commercial and industrial building has moved to a greatness of scale with an amazing acceptance of many modern inventions. This marked advance in extent and quality of post-war construction in fields other than the church places a demand on the church builders that their work shall not recede in comparison, but at least keep step with these developments.

The larger churches built immediately prior to the war or brought to completion following the war, were mostly of stone, and held to traditional patterns. The movement in design appears to be in the direction of much cleaner walls with much simpler detail. The post-war development in these larger buildings may tend to revere historical form, and their character may be influenced by tradition. One feels that an equal or greater beauty could be reached if the designs were more modern and of good proportions, yet of convincing sturdiness (page 122).

**123**

*St. Peter's Church, St. Louis, Missouri. Joseph Murphy, Architect*

*St. Ann's Church, Normandy, Missouri. Joseph Murphy, Architect*

Because of the conditions of the site and the general form which the entire church plant will take as it includes the church, the church school, and other buildings, there will be tremendous variety in the design and composition of the exterior mass. Because of this we can be less definite as to the requirements for the exterior of the modern church than we were concerning the requirements within the church. Those churches which pass beyond the masses required for

*Church of the Resurrection, St. Louis, Missouri. Joseph Murphy, Architect*

their serviceable buildings and include towers, widen still further the possible variations of design (page 123). In each of these, as they develop in the future, we can expect beauty which recalls the fortunate compositions of the past, but solves them in a modern way.

For the most part, the composition of walls and towers as designed by modern architects has a clean appearance which restrains itself within simple geometric form of good proportion. Occasionally, the form passes from the simple and direct construction characteristic of the better modernists of our country to an entirely different treatment of exterior mass such as we find in the La Purisma Church at Monterrey, Mexico. Here the sweep of projecting ribs determines the exterior form of the parabolic church. Such forms attract attention but can scarcely be recommended as suitable solutions. The German churches built in the period following World War I gave us many examples in concrete churches based on the curvature of the parabola. These churches had rather plain exteriors but used the geometric form to simulate medieval vaulting on the interior.

Where such novel forms are used with the dramatic play of buttresses and curved contours, it would seem that further decorative treatment would bring out their dramatic possibilities even though these possibilities are not normal to our choice in church building. If the pattern were well designed, greater interest in the rib-like forms would add to their possible beauty. One would expect a richer architecture, even though its character be very modern, in those countries whose earlier church building was ornamented on nearly every surface. When the desire for such interest accompanies modern building forms they may develop a welcome acceptance. We need not feel that beautiful ornament is a thing of the past. It has nearly become a thing of the past simply because we have so often only copied. Here our skills in creative artistry require courageous development. In the St. Louis Church of the Resurrection (shown above) Joseph Murphy develops an exterior of great simplicity and very appropriate to his plan, which is of parabolic shape. He has managed to unite his tower with the mass of his church, but in a novel position. It is placed on the axis of the plan, at the rear and behind the sanctuary.

A different type of tower arrangement is seen on page 124, St. Ann's Church.

Here we find a very expressive well-proportioned grouping of the masonry church and its tower. The church replaces an earlier church. The tower and chapel, in a remodeled form, continue the memory of the earlier church. Modern church buildings of such good proportion with such excellent use of masonry attract us even though they seem severe in appearance.

This quality of modern masonry is strongly expressed in the exterior walls of the Temple of the Sinai Congregation of Chicago (page 129). By a very direct composition of the lower levels, represented by the foyer at the base of the auditorium, a severe simplicity has been reached. Added interest is created by the choice of materials and the variety of their texture and color.

Paralleling such examples of definitely modern form is the skill and capacity among our modern architects to do refreshing design reflecting traditional pattern. The First Baptist Church at Arlington, Tex., (page 127) Thomas D. Broad, architect, is an excellent example of this position. The facilities of the church and the church school are entirely modern, and advantage has been taken of recent developments for greater usefulness and convenience. In this case the tower has been used in a traditional manner, retaining the position so often chosen in earlier church building. We feel that its composition is fortunate. However, we must remind ourselves that it is appropriate for the modern architect to convince himself concerning this element. Shall our church be built with a tower or without one? Some years ago when writing on this subject I expressed my opinion as follows:

The tower becomes even in the open setting of an open city, the adjunct of a noble church. The church's masonry must have reached adequate dignity and impressiveness before we are justified in the building of a great amount of masonry into a tower expressing our enthusiasm. If the walls need height and solidity, the excess of masonry belongs to them rather than to the tower.*

I find no reason to change my opinion in respect to the tower. The architect, as well as the congregation of the church and the clergy, would enjoy having a tower as part of the scheme of the entire church plan. Whether the tower has any usefulness that would justify its cost is questionable. The additional height gained in the tower expresses at least the traditional composition characteristic of church building, but, until we have done everything we have to do and done it well, we should not spread our means thinly in order to have enough money left to build a tower.

The tower is one of the elements of an entire church plant which often inspires a member of the church to give generously in order to provide a memorial. This is fortunate indeed. The architects would be very glad if it happened more frequently. However, in no manner should the tower and its materials, forms and decorations be allowed to assume an undue importance in the entire mass simply because it is a memorial.

In churches and in educational buildings this has often been a real mistake. The tower will be better, more beautiful, more permanently inspiring to the people if it is the correct, natural and splendid component that brings the church to completion and does not in any way demote or devalue the church itself.

Perhaps this is the time to recall that in modern church building a peculiar substitute has been tried. It is a sort of compromise element, an isolated mass of stone or other masonry. Being more or less shapeless and seldom appropriate, it is like an illuminated sign in commercial work. A bell or a cross may hang on the face of this masonry. When it does, the architect has completed his design. I do not feel that this shows the serious thought and the reverent understanding due the church.

* *Church of Tomorrow*, Harper and Brothers, 1936

*First Baptist Church, Arlington, Texas. Thomas D. Broad, Architect*

Among foreign examples, and occasionally among our domestic ones, light and frail tower forms have appeared which have little relation to the mass of the church. They have openness and lightness from ground to top. In the northern countries of Europe, where they have frequently been used, a large number of the churchmen object to them. It is difficult to see the reasoning behind designs of this character. If it is basic economy, then it would be better to avoid building them at all. The congregation might better wait until it is possible to build them well. If it is not an economy measure, then violent antagonism is expressing itself against churchly forms. The little tower in itself may do no harm. However, the attitude of mind that demands its being there may deliberately distort far more vital churchly meaning.

Having attained good proportions and well conceived simplicity for the exterior mass of our church, we may concentrate our efforts upon the design of the entrance portals. For the church which welcomes in a true sense, the entrance should be neither meagre in material nor minor in scale. Historically, it has been appropriate to develop richness of ornament or scultpure at the church's entrance.

We have two alternatives, based on excellent precedent. One is to treat the entire west front as the portal of the church. The architectural form is then developed to combine the portals with the openings above them into one rich, welcoming unit. The other alternative is to keep the west front simple, rather severe, in good form and proportion, but to concentrate interest entirely at the entrance. In the use of the former approach our modern churches have been fairly well handled, except that the doors have become minor to the point of being insignificant. The reverse was true in splendid work of traditional character. If the church is small and the congregation has few members, a well-shaped entrance consisting of a single pair of doors of good size may be adequate.

A strong yet very simple solution of the entrance doors to a chapel is shown on page 129. The plain brick wall, without ornament, dramatizes the effect. The usual solution to the entrance of the medieval church was a grouping of

*Emanu-El Temple, Houston, Texas. Gabert, MacKie and Kamrath, Architects. Photo by Chalmers-Marvins*

three beautifully proportioned doorways. Such groupings of three doors express welcome and openness. In our modern work, the three doorways are still appropriate, provided our narthex vestibule is spacious. In place of arched openings characteristic of traditional masonry, the modern church chooses to group rectangular openings as one motif. These forms may be combined in a manner that extends throughout the height of the west front with long, vertical window openings over the doors. A very spacious and extremely modern treatment adequate to welcome a very large congregation is shown the Emanu-El Temple in Houston, page 128. Here the horizontal pattern supplants the more usual vertical composition.

The welcoming openness of the west front of the church has been carried to still greater extent in other modern examples. Having the west front entirely of glass is of uncertain value. However, one of the more daring of the examples is that of St. Peter's Church at St. Louis (page 125) where the entire field between the side walls and the roof is a glazed field protected on the interior by screen-like separation of the narthex from the nave.

Sinai Temple, Chicago.
Friedman, Alschuler and
Sincere, Architects.
Grunsfeld, Yerks,
Lichtman and Koenig,
Consulting Architects.
Photo by Hedrich-Blessing

St. Rose of Lima Church,
Houston, Texas.
Donald Bartheleme &
Associates, Architects

*Sculpture Groups,*
*Evangelical Church,*
*Milwaukee, Wisconsin*
*William McVey, Sculptor*

Our modern design of the front of the church has shown but occasional use of sculpture such as marked great churches of the past. It is still at the portals of the church that such richness may be appropriately added. To avoid it is to discard a warm human interest which sensitive skills should embody into church building by means of religious sculpture that is no longer dull imitation. Exquisite sensitiveness and extreme simplicity mark the work of John Angel, sculptor. His figure of the Virgin Mary (below) at the Cathedral of St. John the Divine challenges us to recover these skills.

The serious understanding of sculpture in stone for the exterior of the modern church shows already the recovery of the quality of carving appropriate to the stone upon which the carving is executed. When the portals of the church were first decorated with sculpture at Modena and at Moissac, vigorous and rather primitive modeling seemed appropriate. From such beginnings a vast and rapid development occurred in the sculptures of the portals of the great churches and the cathedrals. Interesting religious groups (shown on opposite page) possessing a very virile quality have been created by the sculptor, William McVey of Cranbook for the Evangelical Church at Milwaukee, Wis. An evolution in sculpture appropriate to the modern church is to be expected as we gain more and more skill in religious arts and we long for sculpture which will develop greater richness and greater dignity at the portals of the modern church.

*The Virgin Mary, Cathedral of St. John the Divine, New York City. John Angel, Sculptor*

# LIGHTING, HEATING AND AIR-CONDITIONING

Church lighting has not kept pace with other elements of modern church building. Advanced modernists still hang rows of glass bowls from the ceiling. Such methods create an impression of makeshift planning which is no better than the Victorian dullness of the past. We must seek a successful mastery of our lighting problems.

Of all the types of pendants that have been used through the long range of history, the simplest was probably the most satisfactory. It consisted of a cylinder of parchment or parchment-colored glass, 2 to 3 ft. long and with a diameter of approximately 12 in. These pendant lanterns afforded a small degree of illumination at the ceiling level, but gave direct light to the congregation through the open bottom of the cylinder. With a sufficient number of these fixtures located in lines placed well above the seating levels, satisfactory modest illumination was achieved.

Just what degree of illumination should be planned throughout the nave area is a matter of diversity of opinion. It would seem that the better churches of the past generation reached only some 3 to 4 foot-candles. Often the measurement was considerably less. There are those among the clergy and the more ritually-minded architects who feel that the dull light is appropriate. We surely do not have occasion to develop a uniform light of approximately 30 foot-candles such as would be used in the interior of modern educational or commercial buildings. A lighting at the pew level which ranges from 6 to 8 foot-candles will serve well. The point, however, is what sort of fixtures we will use and how we will dispose of our lighting units.

One of the simplest and least offensive forms of modern fixture suitable for church use has been the type which is placed above the ceiling. Acoustical blocks have been used as the ceiling treatment in many recent buildings. These blocks can be installed in a series of coffers or panels so as to create a depth and an architectural beauty. Fixtures of the down-light type can be placed so as not to break the pattern and to take no part in the ornamenting of the interior of the nave. When they are lighted, the distribution is or can be made quite uniform. Such fixtures do not distract the congregation as do lines of pendant fixtures. However, this is only a start toward still better schemes for the proper illumination of the church auditorium.

Our plans for the artificial lighting of the nave and chancel might bear a direct relation to the natural light coming through the openings in the walls. We have a most fitting solution if this light is of increasing intensity as we pass from the narthex through the nave to the chancel. Deeper color and darker tones in the stained glass openings at the lower or aisle levels, with less deep tones in the upper or clerestory levels, was characteristic of medieval architecture. At the sanctuary, the number of openings increased the amount of glass, and the windows were larger and more translucent than in the side walls. This was a desirable and intelligent solution, keeping the primacy of the altar as the major interest within the church. We are not likely to use stained glass in its traditional sense in buildings that are of distinctly modern design. Glass of color and glass that is patterned with skill will continue to be used, but not as universally as was the stained glass window of past generations. Fortunately for us, this is a move in the right direction. The stained glass windows tended to create distracting interests and drew the mind as well as the eye of the church-goer from the major interest in the sanctuary, and thus failed to serve the best interests of the church service.

The use of artificial light throughout the nave creates design problems. The very simple cylindrical pendant fixtures solved, to a degree, the lighting for the congregation. They did not illuminate the ceiling or the lofty vaulting levels. They gave only modest general illumination, adequate for circulation through the church. The moderate quantity of light which they shed directly upon those in the pews was the quantity which the traditionalists seemed to feel most appropriate. It is true that the degree of light at the pew level should be increased, but not greatly. Modern lighting units, installed according to commercial practice, whether they are of continuous pattern or located at intervals, tend to illuminate the ceiling to a far greater extent than is correct within the church. Eventual solution of the church lighting problem may be the spot type unit engineered to give uniform light of low intensity at the level of the pews, and retain the darker values of the ceiling surface.

Recessed or hidden cove lighting which is dependent upon configurations in the ceiling has not proved satisfactory. Fixing the greatest illumination at the ceiling level changes the emotional quality of the church at the evening service. Appropriate lighting pattern has resulted from the use of natural light as designed for the daytime service.

A solution to this problem of reconciling natural and artificial lighting has been suggested for churches whose cross-section is a lofty aisle to right and left of the central nave, illuminated with openings adequate to give pleasant lighting over the entire nave. If artificial lighting could be uniformly dispersed in the correct quantity, so that it could come into the nave by night very much as natural light comes into the nave by day, the unity we are trying to reach might be achieved. It would not distract our interest from the chancel. New plans, together with new inventions by electrical manufacturers seeking to meet the architect's need, will develop within reasonable time, and will aid us toward a solution of the problem of church lighting, which up to this time has not been successfully handled.

There was a great deal of merit in the extremely simple pendant fixtures of cylindrical form referred to above. Where the ceiling of the nave was of the open-timber form or of the masonry-vaulted form, the fixture for convenience had to be placed well above the head of the person in the pews, but also well down from the ceiling in order that the lamps might be conveniently replaced. If the lights are raised above the ceiling in the form of the downlight fixture, access must be given to a space above the ceiling for the repair of fixtures and the replacement of lamps. Where the provision for heating and air conditioning is by means of ducts, such space above the ceiling is to be expected and may be used to advantage in serving the lighting fixtures as well as the mechanical elements of the heating and air conditioning system. The greatest disadvantage

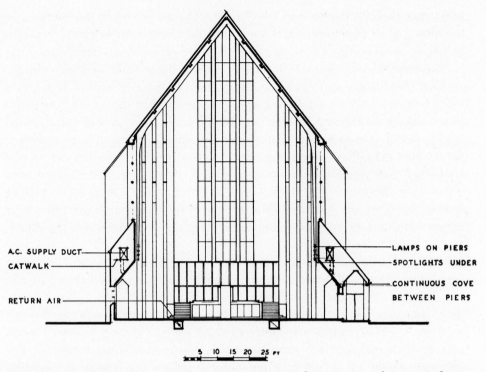

A.C. SUPPLY DUCT
CATWALK

RETURN AIR

LAMPS ON PIERS
SPOTLIGHTS UNDER
CONTINUOUS COVE
BETWEEN PIERS

5  10  15  20  25 FT

*Section Diagram. First Baptist Church, Longview, Texas. Wilson, Morris and Crain, Architects*

of the downlight method is not our inability to get perfect lighting in the correct quantity at the pew level, but rather the possible inclusion of a geometric pattern created by shadows in contrast with strong light projected by the downlamp upon the walls of the nave. If this type of lighting is used, care should be taken to pitch or slant the direction of light so that these shadows are not created upon the walls.

We have had few years since the close of World War II in which to benefit from the amazing skills and studies of electrical nature developed for war purposes. As the church becomes, as it is becoming, one of the major elements of modern building, the architects, with the research engineers, should be able to state their problem clearly and to indicate the degree of lighting which they desire in order to produce the artistic values of their design within the church. It is my opinion that this will be achieved.

From the cross section on this page of a church now in course of building we find solutions providing lighting at the useful level, the lower levels of the nave. There is no lighting from high above. A combination of fixtures forming slender, vertical units at the level of the aisle ceiling is joined with a low degree of continuous lighting at the same level. This is further supplemented by concealed spots correctly directed to cover the nave area. The quantity of lighting has been set at approximately eight candles per square foot. It is expected that the diffused light at this lower level will retain the relatively dark quality of the timber ceiling. The effect by night is similar to that by day.

When we approach the lighting of the sanctuary and chancel of the church, the amount of light per square foot must be increased. It is necessary to have a greater amount of light for the choir, and the light should be greater as we pass toward the sanctuary. The fixtures themselves should not be visible.

When a structural form such as the Arch of Triumph forms the opening from the nave to the chancel, it has been entirely practical to place a series of lights on the chancel side of the arch in a position not visible to the congregation. This adds the greater quantity of lighting required for the choir. While rather practical in its results, it can be unsightly as viewed by the clergy from the altar. Greater refinement of the units and of their architectural treatment would be appropriate.

From similar locations and at properly concealed points, small but effective spot lighting focused directly upon the altar or the baptistry should be provided so that a living interest, created by light, is present on the altar at all times. This brings out the richness of detail of the central motif of the church.

The swivel type spot light has been advantageously used in a number of churches whose ceilings are of either the open-timber or the heavily beamed type. Particularly with the open-timbered ceiling, good results have been obtained by placing the spotlights as high as possible. This provides uniform lighting and the source is not evident to the congregation in the pews. The speaker in the pulpit is at a disadvantage under such conditions. Therefore, lights should be controlled by a rheostat during the sermon period.

The practical difficulties of solving our church lighting without resorting to the pendant type of fixture arise from the great height of the ceiling of the nave and chancel. No fixture is desirable if lamp replacement and repair cannot be done easily. Few churches have available the almost constant mechanical services needed to keep such fixtures in order. They let them become conspicuously out of repair. If fixtures other than the pendant type are to be used, catwalks should be installed to provide easy access for repairs by the usual caretaker of the building. By this means it is possible to keep the lighting system in satisfactory condition.

Exterior lighting for the church front or the church tower is more prevalent than desirable. It is not wrong to give a pleasant flood of light upon the church's entrance or to call attention to the church's emotional form and meaning by the lighting of its tower; it is the manner in which it is done that has been unpleasant. Floodlights placed properly in compliance with engineering practice accomplish the purpose. In the majority of cases the lights themselves are so evident and their appearance so commercial that all good is lost. Low masonry parapets, vine covered walls or an architectural element of some nature suitable to the entire scheme of the church grounds should be used to conceal such purely mechanical developments as exterior floodlights.

Heating and cooling our church requires careful decision. The modern church is incomplete unless it includes an air conditioning system. We in the South speak of it as winter air conditioning and as summer air conditioning. The requirements of our climate have brought about a full acceptance of year-round conditioning as a "must" within the church.

In those climates where reduction of temperature within the church is not required in the summer months, winter conditioning will serve adequately through almost all the year. Even such climates have an occasional season when summer conditioning would be greatly welcomed.

The principal development of this type of heating and cooling has been the delivery and return of air by means of ducts. That modern science and engineering have afforded us the opportunity to maintain clean, healthful temperature and ventilation throughout the entire year, regardless of the cold or hot season, represents a valuable contribution to the church.

We have written at sufficient length concerning the church window, but the conditioned space within the church modifies the importance of the window. The use of movable sections within the stained glass windows was a very unsatisfactory means of ventilation. It created drafts, admitted noises and often appeared unsightly. This was particularly true in lofty windows, such as those of the clerestory. The ventilating panels usually leaked, staining the walls of the church and requiring frequent repair.

**135**

*Chapel, Travis Park Methodist Church, San Antonio, Texas. Henry Steinbower, Architect. Photo by Harvey Patteson & Son*

Heating by means of pipe systems was costly. The radiators, or convectors, did not add to the beauty of the church. With a wide nave they seldom provided uniform heat. The heating was more intense near the side aisles and less adequate near the central aisle. However, uniform distribution was sometimes achieved by skillful engineering and costly construction.

The modern solution which has evolved from such pipe systems as we have been discussing is radiant heating. Many of our modern churches are building their floor slabs directly upon earth fill. A system of radiant heating introduced into the floor slabs in this type of construction proves very economical, and those who have used it report complete satisfaction so far as heating is concerned. While the piping is relatively uniform over the entire area, it is increased along the perimeter near the outside walls and in the narthex area. Such a system is to be recommended in those areas where an air-conditioned building is not sought. It is a system of heating only, and makes no provision for ventilation by conditioned air.

As compared with systems of the past, the simple duct system by which air is filtered and the moisture content properly modified to the desired degree represents a great advance. Air is circulated under pressure through the ducts to openings which give uniform coverage. In a similar manner, the air returns through grilles and ducts to be filtered again with an addition of fresh air in proper proportion. The cost of such installations limited to winter conditioning, which provides circulation and dehumidifying of air throughout the entire year, seems considerably lower than the types used in the past. The major initial cost is for the apparatus necessary to refrigerate the air during the warm season of the year. Initial systems prevailing throughout the South provide the duct system properly insulated for future summer conditioning even though at the time of the installation the machinery required for cooling must be omitted. The maintenance cost of the duct system for winter conditioning is very low. It is

*Large duct located between truss members in roof. Photo by Shoemake-Stiles*

often operated with natural gas as fuel. The greatest consumption of power develops when the refrigerating apparatus is in use.

Each year since the war the cost of installations has decreased. Their universal acceptance is indicated. Still greater savings are to be expected because of the understanding of conditioning as necessary throughout commercial buildings of every character. This will produce wider distribution at lower cost.

In the smaller churches or chapels, the duct system is either carried above the ceiling of the church or furred and plastered in at the angle of the ceiling and the wall (page 134). In the chapel shown opposite the ceiling pattern provides for air conditioning ducts.

In large churches where the area required in the conditioning ducts is much larger, it is most economical to place the ducts above the ceiling. The example shown on this page shows a church which required a seating capacity far in excess of one thousand persons. The large duct was carried between the truss members of the roof. The ceiling was covered with four inches of rock wool to insulate the auditorium against the heat of the attic space. Above the rock wool may be seen continuous wooden platforms or catwalks which give ready access for replacing lamps and provide space for repair or adjustment of the conditioning system.

A modern development for a very large church is indicated in the cross section previously referred to. It is an interesting solution which reminds one of a closed triforium gallery. It consists of a space above the ceiling of the aisle and under the sloping roof above the aisle. The supply ducts are carried throughout the length of the church in this space. Small outlets are placed at each bay interval. The return system is placed under the floor of the aisle as shown in the diagram, with grilles spaced a bay apart. The triforium serves for a repair area, giving access to the lighting system as well as to the air conditioning system. The problem of conditioning the very lofty auditorium of this church is therefore

*Twin compressor units, one carrying 60 per cent of the load, the other 40. Photo by J. D. Burnette*

solved in a somewhat unusual manner. The auditorium height is about 94 ft. at the peak. The nature of the air currents, the tendency of the colder air to fall, and empirical data led to a design of the air distribution system so that the upper strata of air would not be disturbed. Only the lower 40 ft. is conditioned. During the winter heating season the tendency of warm air to rise will prevent stratification to some extent, but the winter heating costs are expected to be much lower than if the plans did not include the use of the upper air for insulation.

The architect and the building committee should be sure to insulate against passage of noise the areas in which the compressors are placed. Efficiency indicates the advantage of placing the compressors as near the auditorium as possible. However, they do create a great deal of noise. Frequently in churches of moderate dimension the compressors are located in a basement area near the chancel end of the church. In such a location the length of the main supply and return ducts will be quite short. The entire surfaces of all the walls and ceiling of the compressor room should be insulated with sound deadening material of at least double thicknesses. Practically noiseless operation, in so far as the auditorium is concerned, has been the result where these precautions were taken.

In air conditioning the auditorium, it is practical to use two compressors of the ratio of 60 per cent and 40 per cent of the total load. These units should be interconnected so as to respond immediately to thermostatic control. The empty church is conditioned quickly by the larger compressor. With the arrival of the congregation, which constitutes the greatest portion of the load, the temperature rises and the second compressor operates automatically. Tests show this to continue for approximately 20 minutes, after which the larger motor is adequate to maintain the temperature and the smaller motor cuts out automatically. The cost of operating the system is less under these conditions.

Where air conditioning as well as heating is provided throughout the church school as well as the church, the architects and engineers should work carefully with the administrative body of the church and the church school to find an economical system. A very large installation would be required to provide simultaneously for a fully-occupied church and all of the rooms of the school. In order to reduce the size of the compressors and thereby the cost of operation, a schedule along the following lines is frequently used: The machines are adequate for the entire conditioning of the school, or for the entire conditioning of the church. The ducts are controlled by dampers. The machinery space for boilers and compressors is arranged as shown in the accompanying view. On Sunday mornings, conditioning is directed into the auditorium of the church at a very early hour. It is then reversed and directed throughout the church school, continuing until approximately 10 or 10:15 A. M. It is then again reversed and directed into the auditorium of the church. If operated with care, this method of reducing initial expense and cost of maintenance is entirely practical.

As we recall the conditions within our older churches and the inconveniences which were often found in church auditoriums of former generations, particularly in regard to lighting, heating and ventilation, we realize how much that makes a modern building modern is in truth scientific advance and development. The term "modern" or "contemporary" as applied to architectural forms of the present day would have been as appropriate at any period of building in man's history. Man can only build as of today. He cannot put together materials in the future, nor is he able to build in the past. The elements which constitute the greatest advances in building, which mark our modern methods, are to a great extent, mechanical developments based on modern science. It is appropriate that the church builders should take every opportunity to use these developments wherever they best serve the purposes of the church building.

# BUILDING THE CHURCH

After the planning stage we come to the work of building our church. In accordance with the usual practice in an architect's office, a limited list of capable, experienced general contractors is chosen. They will be invited to bid on the cost of the work. The choosing of the list of contractors is no more difficult than in any private building enterprise. We seldom encounter more personal opinion or pressure in dealing with our building committee for the church than in dealing with a building committee of a corporation. Frequently there is a contractor whose church affiliations are directly connected with the parish or with the denomination within the city. This should neither penalize nor favor him if the practice of selecting a list of bidders is followed.

In a small percentage of cases the architect may have an opportunity to deal with a single contractor, chosen because of experience, ability, and church connections. If all three fields of his experience are of high repute, it is indeed a pleasant and desirable practice for the church to follow. However, as is usual in architectural experience, especially where the architect is dealing with a large number of owners, there is a preference for competitive bidding.

In church work probably more than in any other type, the personal and individual interest in the process of actual construction is important to many persons, not solely those constituting the building committee.

After the first few experiences in church building, the architect learns to welcome this wide interest during the period of construction. A church in progress of building is often visited once a day by enthusiastic members of the congregation. Some of them feel a personal obligation to be aware of the progress of building.

The architect will be happy if he has insisted steadfastly, during the planning stage, on good materials accompanied by the specification requirements of good workmanship and supervision. Churchmen do not want to see anything shoddy going into their church building. It may have been necessary to exercise economies beyond those which the architect would have chosen. If so, their effects should have been made clear and known to the interested congregation before the plans were finally completed and bids taken.

This does not mean extravagance either in material, workmanship, or detail. It does mean solid, sensible construction which is known to be good, commercially sound, and in no respect inferior. Almost universally, where the facts as to these values are made clear by the architect through the planning stage, he can exclude undesirable material or workmanship from his documents.

140

The members of the building committee usually follow, with considerable regularity, the progress at the building from the first arrival of materials until the final completion. Because of the variety of experience and knowledge within the committee, the items of material or construction that develop their individual interest vary. Taking the entire range of the committee, the architect is very likely to find hardly a single field, no matter how minor, which is not represented by some moderate knowledge and some limited experience on the part of a committee member.

Because of this wide interest in church building, the architect is likely to encounter a large number of suggestions and requests for change in items required by the drawings and specifications. He should take the time to explain carefully the reasons governing decisions made in the planning stage. If this is done in an entirely friendly and courteous manner, such suggestions will result in fewer changes than would be normal in a commercial job. Here again experience is the architect's best armor.

I can recall numerous instances in which those who made seemingly important suggestions, divergent from the plans, became still more interested when the reasons for the practices and designs required by the drawings were clearly defined and enthusiastically presented by the architect. This courtesy resulted in building up an enthusiasm among the laymen for the method the architect had chosen.

In view of this daily interest in the building's progress, the architect should provide in his specifications insistence upon orderliness and cleanliness around the job at all stages of the work. Such conditions are desirable in all building, but they are more important in church building than in other fields.

The purpose of these suggestions is to make clear that there exists an attitude of mind among those who are directly responsible and those who are not so directly responsible in the building of the church to feel a deep sense of obligation as well as of opportunity. This comes from the finer elements of humanity developed by the teachings of the church. Building is a direct opportunity, causing laymen to feel their personal religious obligation.

The sense of service so universally demonstrated by the church members during the period of church building is felt because for them this is likely to be their one opportunity to take part in the building of a church. They look upon this particular church as a permanent building which will serve throughout the lifetime of their children and their children's children. Intimacy of meaning becomes personal as well as communal. We regret that there are not more churches to be built so that more men may take part in their building and reap the benefits of such understanding.

As the building progresses, the foundations have been placed, and the floor slab of the nave completed as far as the rough slab is concerned, it is usual to make arrangements for laying the cornerstone. This ceremony is a service of more importance and generally planned with more care than the usual ceremony of cornerstone laying in buildings of other types. Provision for a larger number of participants must be arranged. The site around the position of the cornerstone needs clearing of unused materials. Precautions must be taken to insure reasonable safety against injury or accident. A sufficient number of competent employees of the contractor should be available to watch the movement of members and caution them of any possible danger. As the service is a solemn one and signifies the reality of building, suggestions by the architect which will enhance the orderly planning and execution of the preparations are very appropriate. Often the architect can help by his facility of design to complete a program that is more beautiful and dignified because of his personal efforts in cooperation with the clergy and the committees responsible for the ceremony.

**141**

By the time the building has reached the stage of the cornerstone setting, the qualities of the contractor will have become very apparent. The work becomes more important each day with regard to the care with which it is done and the complete understanding of the materials and workmanship vital to refined results. If we have been fortunate enough to secure a contractor with experience in the field of church building, and one whose work has been of a high standard, we should encourage even a higher standard by sustaining the maximum enthusiasm of the contractor. If the contractor, though capable in a business and commercial sense, has had but little experience in church building, the architect or his superintendent, usually both of them, should make it a point to give advice gained from earlier experiences, so as to make more smooth the contractor's problems at the building. Time can be saved, disappointments avoided, and above all the fact will be made clear at the outset that the job is to be one representing good workmanship.

Almost as much enthusiasm in church building can be built up among the workmen on the job as among the congregation. Such enthusiasm extends through the various levels of labor and creates a feeling of pride in the work. Workmen, too, recognize that the church is a building of permanent meaning, and that their workmanship will endure to prove that it has a greater meaning than similar elements of work on commercial structure.

Arbitrary decision without cooperation tends to invite dispute. There should be no occasion of either arbitrary decision or dispute in church building, provided it is approached along the lines suggested.

As the building reaches a stage of progress where its form is fully apparent, suggestions and often gifts appear. The growing interest makes it possible for members of the committee or the clergy to visualize further beauty of material or design that might be reached before there is any duplication or waste, provided additional means were given. The fact that the position which the material and its workmanship will occupy is clear to the layman, aids greatly in getting such results. While they cause the architect a loss of time and additional drawing, they make possible a more nearly perfect building. Therefore, when such suggestions appear to be timely, it is very sensible to present them to best advantage and to welcome their acceptance, even though some additional work may be involved that may be inconvenient for the architect's office.

Because of the cooperative participation of the members of the congregation as well as the committee, it is important that accounting records be kept up to date and the committee be kept informed of the financial status. The business practices of the church financial office are, on the average, about the same in their efficiency as those of private clients or of the smaller commercial institutions. The manner of professional accounting, issuing of change orders, issuing of certificates to contractors, etc. is necessarily somewhat new to a church committee. They usually aren't acquainted with it. If the items are made clear to the financial authorities of the church at the start and kept up-to-date throughout the entire progress, it is likely that there will be as complete understanding as from any other clients the architect encounters.

Church congregations and their committees are far less willing to chance financial uncertainty than they were 20 or 30 years ago. Commitments, where loans are required, are usually made in advance of their need, and the extent of these commitments fully determined. The committee, with the architect, makes every effort to stay safely within the limits so prescribed. We make note of this item of church building purely as a result of many experiences in which precaution taken continuously did safely avoid pitfalls. The contractors in order to progress rapidly and to secure prompt deliveries, must receive their payments when they come due as prescribed by the contract. The architect can aid the committee

**142**

by placing before them a schedule of expected monthly requirements and their amounts. These can be still more accurate if checked with the contractor and placed at the possible maximum rather than the minimum.

The contract for the building consists of either a single contract covering the general contract and all mechanical contracts, or a general contract with separate contracts for the plumbing, the heating and air conditioning, the electrical work, and other minor contracts. The completion of these contracts does not constitute the completion of the church. Unlike many private contracts where the furniture and equipment (that is, movable equipment) may be purchased entirely by the owner, the furnishings and fixtures for the church are or should be part of the architect's work. Their manufacture, delivery, and installation should be completed before we consider the church brought to completion.

This equipment should be ordered so that its arrival will coincide with the closing stages of the building contractor's work. Nothing can be more disappointing than to have undue delay arise from failure to design and contract for the furnishing early enough to allow adequate time for its manufacture by capable companies. The congregation becomes very anxious, as its church appears nearly completed. The people want to enjoy its useful and beautiful spaces. For this reason the architect, clergy, and the committee in charge should give serious consideration to the importance of the furnishings. They should resist to the utmost any effort to temporize, or to shift to unsightly furnishings taken for temporary use either from an old church or secured in some other manner. The effect of such makeshift is usually to destroy the enthusiasm that has been reached by the congregation during the building period.

# FURNISHING THE CHURCH

The welcoming grace expressed within our church will be in proportion to the good taste shown in the design of its furnishings. The picture which we see on entering the church is not composed entirely of its beautifully designed structure. The well-shaped forms which prevail throughout the nave, beautiful materials skillfully used for its walls and ceilings, and greater dignity in the composition of the chancel—all of these form but part of the ensemble. The view which faces us should be an inspiring one. The dignity at the altar end of the vista must be one of refinement, and of spiritual meaning.

Composed around that central point will be the furniture necessary for the complete service of that particular church. These pieces must have richness in proportion to their proximity to the altar, and with diminishing richness and ornament as we pass from the sanctuary into the nave.

The largest element in quantity is the furniture for the pews of the church. The wooden bench always traditional in the churches of England, has continued to be the prevailing type used in our most modern churches. The wooden bench represents orderliness and formality, almost regimentation. The degree of comfort developed by such seating is minimal.

Very real adjustments and improvements of the contour of the wooden seat and back of the church pew have been developed, but at best they do not give complete comfort to many of the members of the congregation.

The architect's interest as well as that of the church committee has tended to use heavy ends on the pews. Many of us can recall the rich Gothic pew ends, which were higher than necessary and terminated with a carved finial, or other device; we also remember the softly rolling curves of heavy form used in churches of Georgian or Renaissance tradition which were similar to the graceful curves of the Roman bench end. Others will recall the closed type Colonial pew of New England with its panelled pew door which was opened by the usher only to admit the rightful tenants. Each of these various patterns exemplified the high skills of carpentry prevailing at their particular time. They were usually of splendid material. They seemed to outlast true usefulness and to perpetuate needlessly a good bit of discomfort.

A sensitive understanding of what was suitable in both richness of material and degree of ornamentation began to develop in American churches about 1910. Much of the ornament, much of the panelled nature of the pew ends was abandoned. In place of the more ornamental type, simple rectangular ends with or without ornament were substituted. If ornament was used, it was

**144**

*Christ Evangelical Lutheran
Church, Minneapolis, Minnesota.
Saarinen, Saarinen &
Associates, Architects.
Photo by George Ryan Studios*

*Chapel, Travis Park
Methodist Church, San Antonio,
Texas. Henry Steinbower,
Architect. Photo by
Harvey Patteson & Son*

*Small Chapel, Conventual Church of St. Mary and St. John, Cambridge, Massachusetts. Cram and Ferguson, Architects. Photo by Haskell*

limited in area; a small, sunken panel of symbolic form. This much plainer pew end did a great deal to dignify the picture within the church as compared with the ornamental forms that had preceded it.

It is entirely appropriate that a piece of furniture so necessary as the church pew should tempt the modern architect to seek new forms, improvements on those of the immediate past. In this search interesting forms have appeared. The open-railed back is in my opinion a little too informal and certainly rather uncomfortable as compared with the solid back. With the open-railed back the rough carpentry pew end further reduces the dignity of the pew. Among the cleanest and most beautiful forms of pew ends and backs in recent work are those to be found in Saarinen's Christ Evangelical Lutheran Church in Minneapolis (page 145). There the pew ends are extremely simple and afford the maximum of convenience. The entire pew suggests forms appropriate to strong lasting furniture developed with understanding of carpentry skills.

The individual chair form so frequently to be seen in the cathedrals of Europe

*East Liberty Presbyterian Church, Pittsburgh, Pennsylvania. Cram and Ferguson, Architects. Photo by Haskell*

was not without merit. Occasionally, we find it in use in the American church, particularly in smaller churches or in chapels (page 146). Its design has been of rigid severity, probably because of cost. Good furniture patterning could easily improve the design of such units. The disadvantage of the individual chair is that it requires a larger amount of seating area within the church to

**147**

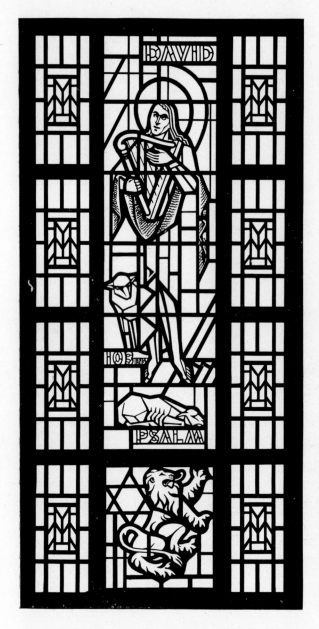 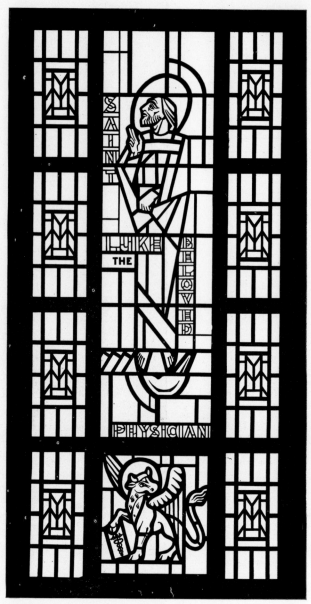

accommodate the same number of members. The width per chair is greater than the width required per person seated in the church pew. Another disadvantage is that the chair is not usually fastened to the floor. It may be moved from one location to another readily. As a result, considerable labor is required to replace, realign and respace the chairs in regular order. This inconvenience as well as the added cost of the furniture itself and of the space required for it, has prevented the chair from coming into wide or universal use.

The more modern types of auditorium seatings which provide comfort and convenience have had but little acceptance in church use. They represent a field of furniture building that should be thoroughly studied for design in order that the practical advantage might be accepted and the commercial appearance completely discarded. The best of such units do afford great convenience, comfort and quiet. Their use within churches, where they have been used, has gained favor. While more costly per seating than church pews, they do not require additional area within the church in order to accommodate the same number of seatings. Where used, they have afforded much easier entrance into the seating rows than was possible in entering the wooden pew. This is a

*Windows by Henry Lee Willet. Methodist Hospital Chapel, Houston, Texas.*
*Watkin, Nunn, McGinty & Phenix, Architects*

great convenience. The opportunity is waiting for skillful designers to perfect the type of church seating affording the maximum comfort, dignity, and quiet fitting to the church use. There is no reason to adhere to either the traditional or to the crude modern bench forms. Such adherence cannot be supported purely by stubbornness, any more than the commercial forms can be accepted as suitable for church use. The question poses a problem appropriate to the advancing of the skills and arts dealing with the furniture of the church.

Greater beauty can be achieved in the furnishing of the church if the simpler characteristics of modern design are reflected in the pattern of the stained glass windows. Many modern windows are of rectangular shape rather than the traditional arch shapes. This plainer form requires sensitive selection of the pattern in the window, though it continues to invite rich deep color and heavy vertical leading. The window designers must express religious meaning with great clarity. Modern window design seems to insist on a purposeful departure from traditional form in order to avoid conflict and to unify walls, windows and furnishings.

The three large windows shown are to be placed in a modern chapel which

*Altar, St. Rose of Lima Church, Houston, Texas. Donald Barthelme & Associates, Architects. Photo by Burt Moritz*

serves a general hospital. The central window shows the figure of St. Luke, while those to the right and left show the figures of Dorcas and of David. The backgrounds are countercharged with blues and golds. From designs of such merit one may gain a vista of future windows which, possessing both thoroughness of workmanship and brilliance of color, will add to the richness of our furnishings.

Besides the matter of seating, the furnishings normal to the church consist of the richer and more spacious stalls of the choir area, the enclosing rails at the face of the chancel, the lectern, the pulpit and the chairs for the clergy. These normally occupy the choir section of the chancel. Beyond them, within the sanctuary, in certain churches, the furnishings consist of the Communion rail, the Bishop's chair, the Sedalia, the Credence and the Altar. As the baptistry is a structural form built with the church, we could hardly include it as furniture.

The degree of richness in material and ornament in the chancel furniture is greater than that of the seating within the nave, but less than that within the sanctuary. We are or should be building up our entire picture to create a maximum central interest at the altar (page 145).

The illustrations in this section show examples of the arrangement and design of furnishings within the sanctuary as they have been developed within recent years. These examples range from small, inexpensive churches to churches of great dimension. They also include recently built churches of traditional as well as of modern design.

*Baptistry, Calder Baptist Church, Beaumont, Texas. Wirtz, Calhoun & Tungate, Architects. Photo by Drew*

For instance, the arrangement of the sanctuary in the chapel of St. Rose of Lima (page 150) is extremely simple. The altar is placed in the usual position in the sanctuary area. Practically all of the examples chosen hold to this central position of either the altar or the baptistry. Beyond this uniformity the examples are diverse in material, dimension, and ornament.

It is my opinion that the reader will find his preference is for directness and simplicity provided the altar or baptistry reaches adequate dimension and is in proportion to the size of the church. Too often an altar which is beautiful in design and of excellent material is too small to reach the perfection it should attain. By means of the dorsal or the reredos its primacy can be enhanced, but not fully attained if the altar is of insufficient length.

The furnishing of the sanctuary of a church in which the baptistry occupies the focal point is necessarily difficult. If the baptistry is slightly raised, an altar can be placed in front of it. This has proved to be an attractive arrangement. When the baptistry is raised to considerable height, it may prove more dramatic, but seems to lose its primacy of meaning. As viewed from the congregation, the ceremonies of baptism seem much more completely expressed if the baptistry is the true center of interest in the sanctuary. Such a solution has been done in a very dignified manner in the Chapel of the Calder Baptist Church of Beaumont, Tex. (above). The design is Georgian, the proportions are very pleasant, and certainly the interest is excellently centered on the bapistry rather than on the pulpit.

Those churches which follow the traditions of Colonial architecture depend largely on the delicacy of their detail because of the uniformity of color or lack of color. Unless the detail is of an intimate type, the churches seem cold. They

*Chancel, Presbyterian Church, New Rochelle, New York. Eggers and Higgins, Architects. Photo by Gottscho Schleisner*

often lack the welcoming quality which was true in the work of the eighteenth century when a wealth of detail characterized the churches of this type.

The very beautiful interior view of the sanctuary of the New Rochelle Presbyterian Church shows clearly the cleanliness of such an interior and the satisfying simplicity of form which is dignified but avoids even the suggestion of bareness. Possibly we restrict ourselves too much as to color, particularly in the sanctuary. When the treatment consists of rich choir stalls of oak, elaborate altar, reredos, and stained glass windows, the warmth is recovered. With the far greater simplicity indicated in modern work we will find that unless color is introduced, there is a feeling of inadequacy, almost of bareness.

In a small chapel which I designed a few years ago, I chose to use considerable color in its furnishing. The altar and triptych (page 153) were of excellent oak, heavily coated with gold leaf. The backgrounds of all carving were in color with polychrome color glazes applied to the carving itself. The result was very quiet, in no sense gaudy. Color seemed to give the needed life and warmth to the work.

The position of the altar in the sanctuary has come to be accepted in the sense of the English tradition. It is placed at the eastern wall. The altar may have additional depth because of the reredos, but is essentially at the very end of the interior. I am surprised that the more modern designs have not chosen to bring to the altar the distinction of standing free from the eastern wall. This has been done consistently in the churches of Roman Catholic faith. The space behind the altar may be modest or large. If the altar is of the canopy type, treated with a baldachino, it is naturally freed from the east wall. Richer possibilities are obtainable if greater space is allowed for the sanctuary. The position of the altar and baldachino shown in the Church of St. Peters (page 155) records the preference in Catholic churches for adequate openness in the planning of the sanctuary. This arrangement provides very generous depth beyond the altar.

When we consider the practical problems of the women of Altar Guilds as they perform their service, we see what an advantage it would be to have a more ready means of access to the altar and retable shelf than is normally true. Compositions for depth in flower arrangements would be welcome and could be handled with great beauty.

In contrast to the more open solution indicated above, the practices within the reader's church may be those which do not require depth behind the altar. In these churches greater dimensions and fitting enrichment are invited by a reredos treatment. By means of the reredos sufficient dimension can be obtained to create the proper feeling. In too many instances where the reredos has been the treatment used, it has been too small. It was neither wide enough nor high enough to fulfill its purpose. The cost of a splendidly designed reredos is considerable, and possibly because it costs so much its dimensions have been reduced in order to effect a saving. If we are to plan a reredos, let us set the correct dimensions first and avoid excessive ornament so as to be able to

*Chapel, Christ Church Cathedral, Houston, Texas.*
*William Ward Watkin, Architect.*
*Photo by Cecil Thompson Studio*

*Conventual Church of St. Mary and St. John, Cambridge, Massachusetts. Cram and Ferguson, Architects. Photo by Haskell*

purchase a reredos of adequate dignity and in proper proportion to the dimensions of our sanctuary. The conventual church of St. Mary and St. John, Cambridge, Mass. (above), is an example where proper dimensions produce the proper effect of the altar and its canopy. The treatment is of excellent material, very simple in its design and rich in color.

The sanctuary within the Jewish temple has unique meaning because of the primacy of the Ark of the Covenant. The dramatic possibilities of composition are abundant. One of the handsomest examples I have seen is that of the Emanu El Temple of San Francisco. The entire building is a very beautiful one. It is within the temple that the whole composition seems to be wonderfully dramatized. The composition (page 155) shows that religious reality can be made clear and vibrant. The fact that the grouping stands free from the apse wall gives it still greater fullness.

**154**

*St. Peter's Church, St. Louis, Missouri. Joseph Murphy, Architect*

Modern and less traditional solutions also seek dramatic interest. The sanctuary shown on page 156 is such an example. This treatment is consistent with the simple interior. Its color is restrained and its effect is pleasant though rather severe.

A very impressive example of modern design is to be found in the Temple of the Sinai Congregation in Chicago (page 158). This design adequately expresses the proper size, richness and simplicity typical of the trend in all of our churches.

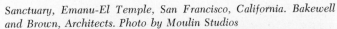

*Sanctuary, Emanu-El Temple, San Francisco, California. Bakewell and Brown, Architects. Photo by Moulin Studios*

*Sanctuary, Emanu-El Temple, Houston, Texas. Gabert, MacKie and Kamrath, Architects. Photo by Chalmers Marvins*

This philosophy declares religious meaning by focalizing interest in either the altar, the ark, or the baptistry according to the practices of the church.

Two outstanding creations of ecclesiastical art of the past generations are the work of Maginnis and Walsh, architects, of Boston. In each instance their fine artistry raised to true meaning the chancel of the churches in which these great works were placed.

There are still some of us who recall very clearly the chancel of Trinity Church, Boston, as it was at the beginning of this century. Richardson's great church was a monument to the architecture of the latter half of the nineteenth century. The chancel was rather formless in its furnishings. There was no conviction of purpose. It was broad, high, open, yet void. As we see it today (page 157) with beauty of treatment designed by the Maginnis firm, great unity has been developed. The beauty of the apse form has been raised to dominate the interior. Religious art with worthy craftsmanship has ennobled the sanctuary. As a result of this splendid work, the entire character of the interior of Trinity Church has reached a correct fulfillment.

*Altar, Trinity Church, Boston, Massachusetts. Maginnis and Walsh, Architects. Photo by Andre Snow*

*Sanctuary, Sinai Temple, Chicago. Friedman, Alschuler and Sincere, Architects; Grunsfeld, Yerks, Lichtmann and Koenig, Consulting Architects. Photo by Hedrich-Blessing Studio*

More glorious still is the work done by the same firm at St. Patrick's Cathedral in New York City. Vast spaces, great beauty, the wealth of tradition, that exist within the sacred shadows of the cathedral require a corresponding beauty in the furnishing of the sanctuary. Those of us who recall the treatment of the sanctuary as it existed before the work of Maginnis and Walsh, know our impression of incompleteness. The depth of the sanctuary was denied. The distances within the sanctuary and on into the Lady Chapel were blocked by the low, wide reredos. The reredos was of white marble in elaborate Gothic form, repeating itself again and again. In combination with the altar, it formed a low wall contrasting unfavorably in color and of excessive ornament. With the replacement of the older treatment of the sanctuary by the marvelous slender forms of the new altar and baldachino, the church seems recreated. The purity of the Gothic grandeur within the church is no longer confused or denied (page 159). Towering nearly 60 ft. from the floor, the combination of marble high altar and bronze baldachino embody those inherent spiritual qualities which are in truth the spirit of the church. In no example that I have seen at home or

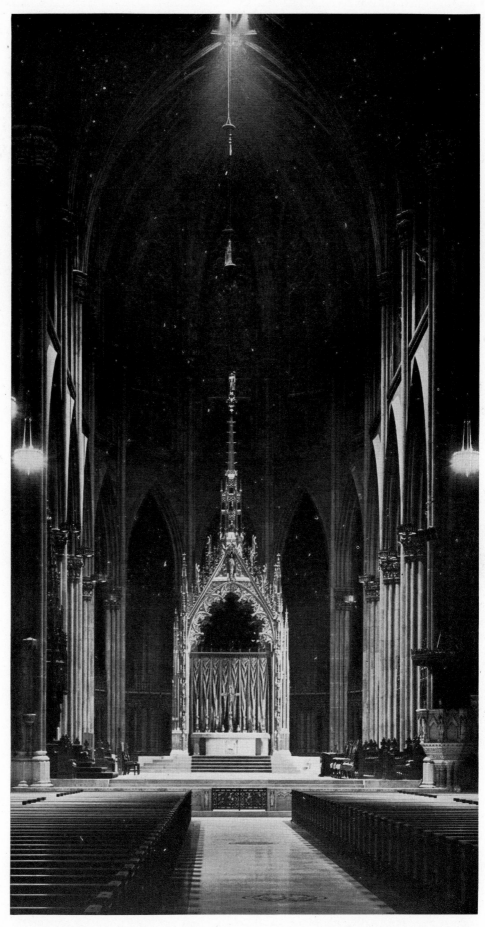

*Altar and Baldachino, St. Patrick's Cathedral, New York City. Maginnis and Walsh, Architects. Photo by Gottscho-Schleisner*

abroad has there been such complete artistry and recovery of religious inspiration as has been accomplished in this grand work.

It is indeed a magnificent service to the church and to the architecture of the church that has been rendered by Charles D. Maginnis and by the sculptor, John Angel. Glorious as this altar and baldachino appear by day, they become even more ethereal when viewed by night, when the loftiness of the cathedral seems even greater than by day, and the towering slenderness of the baldachino with its sculpture becomes as a vision rather than a reality.

In these days of continued strife within the social structure of nations and with uncertainty dimming, as by a great impenetrable fog, the clear perspective of the mind of man, we approach the church and its altar as the one eternal security. Here men have found throughout all ages consolation, comfort, and courage. The years and the centuries throughout which the church grew to majestic position in architecture were neither years nor centuries of peace. Man's effort was continuous toward a social structure that would maintain peace within the world, yet each successive step failed of perfection. This is no less true today, but our comfort in the warm assurance of the church's meaning does not prevail as completely as it did in those bygone times. This is probably the most vital recovery that civilization throughout the world needs today. For the architects, the clergy and the laymen of the world there rises a tremendous challenge to tireless effort that the church may be again primary in our civilization and that it may be so expressed. From the traditions of the Middle Ages, with their pattern and promise of a way of life, much appears to have passed from our manner of thought. In war or in peace a Christian civilization can find solution only by recalling that solution requires the quality of justice and that justice must be understood as a quality of the will of God. So in a symbolic manner let us hope that when the problems of peace persist, there shall be seen by all men a symbol above all and visible to all. That symbol shall not be one of narrow meaning. In the simple geometry of the cross it shall represent, not boundaries of creed, but universal understanding and justice. It shall be the symbol of justice which is the eternal quality of the church, the will of God, a symbol that will lead men to create beautifully and not to destroy recklessly.